AMERICAN RED CROSS

FIRST AID TEXTBOOK
FOR
JUNIORS

This textbook has been written for the American Red Cross by Carl J. Potthoff, M.D., M.P.H., National Director of First Aid and Associate Medical Director. The illustrations were prepared by Mary Allen Hood, Ruth K. Macrae, and William Brown McNett. The American Red Cross acknowledges with deep appreciation the contribution made by educational, medical, and safety leaders and by its own administration and technical staff members, who have read the manuscript and made many useful suggestions.

AMERICAN RED CROSS

FIRST AID TEXTBOOK
FOR
JUNIORS

THE BLAKISTON COMPANY · PHILADELPHIA

PRINTED IN THE U. S. A., BY J. W. CLEMENT CO., BUFFALO, N. Y.

TYPESETTING BY THE NORTH AMERICAN COMPOSITION CO., INC., PHILADELPHIA, PA.

SUGGESTIONS FOR INSTRUCTORS

This textbook is intended for use in teaching first aid in schools and other organizations to students who are 12, 13, or 14 years old or are in the seventh, eighth, or ninth grade. Older students should take the Standard First Aid Course.

The American Red Cross offers, as a further service, a plan whereby class members may be granted Red Cross Junior First Aid Certificates upon completion of the course. Use of the plan, where feasible and desired, may help foster interest, study, and favorable attitudes among the students. Certificated courses, which are taught by authorized instructors, may be presented as a separate subject in a school curriculum or as a part of a broader subject. In 1948 the Red Cross modified its requirement for the authorization of professional teachers and adopted a policy of reauthorizing, upon request in later years, and without further requirement, any teacher who continues in professional educational work. Thus, under present policy, if a teacher is once authorized, her class members in future years will be granted Red Cross certificates if she requests reauthorization and reports the class members as having passed the Junior First Aid Course. Information concerning the plan may be obtained from the local Red Cross chapter.

OBJECTIVES OF FIRST AID TEACHING

At the junior level, the most important objective of first aid teaching is accident prevention, applied safety-mindedness. The approach made to safety in this way is an oblique one, but general observation and many statistical studies show that it is very effective. For example, in many industries that carry on a diversified attack against accidents, those people who receive first aid education show a reduction of 30 to 50 percent in accidents compared with others who do not receive first aid training, though doing the same kind of work and receiving the same safety education otherwise. Such first aid education bears fruit indefinitely because the recipient typically has a favorable attitude toward further safety education and admonition.

In an average year about fifteen thousand young people, age 5 through 19, die from accidents; and almost one and one-half million suffer disabling injuries. The problem must be attacked on many fronts, and any method that promises a significant reduction in a toll like this deserves use. The educator, of course, has a key role in safety work.

The second objective of first aid education is to teach what to do and what not to do in case of accident or sudden illness. This education will find use many times, often when the need for it is great.

INTEGRATION

The various units of study in this textbook provide opportunities for comprehensive integration with other junior high school courses and with life situations. In each unit there is first a discussion and practical work session, designed primarily to present the heart of a first aid topic and to relate the subject matter to life experiences. An extensive list of problems, playlets, and things to do is included in the units.

Integration with English is developed through problems and assignments in writing narratives, descriptions, and expositions, in dictionary use, vocabulary building, playlet and radio script writing, and in acting. Combined assignments in English and first aid can therefore be given.

Integration with citizenship or civics courses is provided through problems aimed to give familiarity with official organizations such as fire, police, health, and welfare departments, and with other civic groups. The relationship of accidents to poverty, unemployment, and welfare problems is considered in many units, particularly unit 5. It is hoped that the discussions and various problems will contribute toward developing social-mindedness and instilling a desire to participate in community affairs. Integration with art is possible through poster-making work. Accident statistics studies can extend to arithmetic problems and graph making.

The great objective of all health education is improved behavior in everyday living. If the teaching situation conforms closely to the real life situation, the carry-over may be good. In these units of work, playlets dramatizing accident scenes are presented, and practical skills work is emphasized. Such features in a course add interest, promote favorable attitudes, provide student activity, and give emphatic visual teaching. In presenting "things to do" at home, considerable attention is directed to farm safety and first aid. Anything that the junior course teacher can do to reach farm people with education in safety and first aid is worth while.

C. J. P

THE CERTIFICATING COURSE

The development of safety-mindedness to the point of improving behavior requires *build-up*. The student who in many lessons learns about fractures, burns, concussion, and other injuries, who notes the personal disasters that they represent, the impact upon the community, and the fact that these disasters happen to people of his own age and group, develops this true safety-mindedness. The objective of safety-mindedness is not so effectively gained by merely presenting a few lectures on selected first aid topics.

An over-all picture of first aid equips the student better for knowing what to do in case of injury. The student will benefit somewhat from study of a few topics such as artificial respiration and control of bleeding. But in many accidents the injury is not revealed readily. The first aider must be prepared to meet various injuries. The problems of general procedure at an accident, of examination of victims, or transportation need, dangers, and method often are completely overlooked when only a half dozen lessons are devoted to first aid. Further, if only a few lessons are presented, practical work is often entirely omitted. The certificating course or its equivalent is therefore better than the occasional lecture for developing safety-consciousness and for preparing students to know what to do and what not to do in case of accident.

Certificating classes should complete all the discussions and practical work, but the teacher assigns or omits problems and things to do as class needs and time suggest. By presenting the theory and practical work in each unit up to the point marked thus, _____ (see page 4), the teacher fulfills the minimum requirements toward Red Cross certification. The material presented thereafter in each unit is optional. Each unit has been designed to present practical work based on the discussion in that unit when feasible. In those units in which no applicable skills are required, material has been inserted to augment discussions in previous units. This applies to both practical work and optional teaching aids. It has been found desirable to extend the teaching of some skills through several units even though the related theory is presented in only one unit.

Each unit is designed to represent one lesson of about 45 minutes. A useful time allocation for a lesson is 25 or 30 minutes for review and presentation of the lesson topic and problems, and 20 minutes for practical skills work. Lesson time allocations are only suggested; however, students should not be reported for certificates unless they have had adequate practice on skills in class and have completed the theoretical work satisfactorily. Generally speaking, teacher demonstration should precede the students' practical skills work.

Authorized instructors of the certificating course can obtain a free copy of the *First Aid Instructor's Manual* (ARC 1019) from the local Red Cross chapter. This manual provides many teaching helps.

When classes are reported for certification, *Examination Record—Junior First Aid Course* (Form 325B) should be used. The completed record in duplicate is sent to the local Red Cross chapter. Information concerning examining and grading is given in the form.

MATERIALS NEEDED

Materials for use by the teacher:

Several triangular bandages.

Specimens of 4-tailed and roller bandages for demonstration purposes.

Specimens of dressings, preferably of various sizes and kinds, for demonstration purposes.

Charts showing the human circulatory, respiratory, and skeletal systems. (A single first aid instruction chart containing the essential information is available. The local Red Cross chapter may provide one, or will sell one for a nominal sum.)

A first aid kit, if possible.

Materials for use by class members:

1 triangular bandage for each student in class.

Blankets, mats, or newspapers for use as floor covering when practicing splinting, artificial respiration, and transportation.

2 stretcher poles, if possible.

Splints about 3 x 17 inches and from one-eighth to one-quarter of an inch thick; 1 splint per student.

Gauze compresses, various sizes; 1 for every 2 students.

The above is a suggested list and may be modified according to class size. The triangular bandages may be made by the class. A square of 40-inch muslin, cut diagonally, makes 2 bandages. Splints may be made from light wood—packing boxes, orange crates, and the like. Compresses may be made from cheesecloth or any other cloth. Paper handkerchiefs or folded newspaper will do if cloth is not available. Of course, these make-believe compresses are not actually sterile, but should be handled in all bandage practice as though they were.

CONTENTS

REFERENCE MATTER

1

NEED FOR
FIRST AID; SHOCK

What Is First Aid?

First aid is the immediate care given to an injured or sick person until the services of a physician can be obtained.

Value of Having First Aid Knowledge

If you know how to give first aid properly, you are able to help others when they need help most. When someone is injured, people are always willing to help. But often, because they have not studied first aid, they make mistakes and injure the victim even more. The good first aider knows what to do and also what not to do.

By giving proper care you may save lives or prevent lifelong crippling. You will decrease suffering and perhaps cause the accident or illness expenses to be less than they otherwise would be. Many young people have become heroes because they knew what to do in case of drowning, injuries, bleeding, and so on. Another important result of studying about accidents is that you become more careful and have fewer accidents yourself.

The Cost of Accidents

You will probably see a serious accident some time. In 1948, in this country, there were more than 10 million accidents serious

1

enough to cause loss of time from regular activities for more than one day. One hundred thousand people—as many as there are in the city of Duluth—died of these accidents, and many more suffered permanent injuries. The total cost was more than 6½ billion dollars, or enough to give every eighth-grade student in the United States that year about $3,000. Instead, the money went for accident costs.

The greatest cause of death among people between the ages of 2 and 27 years is not pneumonia, tuberculosis, or any other disease; it is accidents. Most of the accidents that cause serious injuries are preventable. Many are caused by carelessness, by recklessness, or by ignorance.

SHOCK

What Is Shock?

When a person is badly injured, he may develop a serious condition called shock. In shock cases, the blood flow in the body is disturbed, even in parts distant from the injury. The brain does not get enough blood. Thinking is difficult, digestion of food is slowed, and all body processes are at a low level. The injured person feels exceedingly weak. Unless he receives proper care, he may die of shock, or his recovery may be greatly delayed.

Causes of Shock

Any serious injury may cause shock. Bad burns, loss of much blood, broken bones, and large cuts are often followed by shock. Shock may also occur because of serious illness. Emotional disturbance sometimes leads to a temporary state of shock. During the last war millions of Americans gave some of their blood through the Red Cross for use by doctors in treating shock resulting from war wounds.

Signs of Shock

The skin of a person in shock feels cool and is whiter than usual. Sometimes perspiration appears, especially on the forehead or chin, or above the mouth. Sometimes the victim feels like vomiting or actually does vomit.

First Aid for Shock

Whenever you give first aid to a seriously injured person, always try to prevent shock. Act immediately. Do not wait for shock to appear.

Make the victim lie down at once, so that his head is level with or lower than the rest of his body. However, if his breathing in this position is difficult because of chest injuries, raise the head and shoulders by placing pillows under them.

Cover him properly. Carefully place a blanket under him. If the weather is not hot, place a coat or blanket over him. If the weather is very cold, use several blankets. But don't make him sweat; too much covering is undesirable.

Ordinarily you should not use hot water bottles or electric heating pads on accident victims. However, you may use them if the weather is very cold and there aren't enough blankets. The best places to use them are under the armpits or about the chest. Take care not to burn the skin.

Give warm water to drink if an hour or more will pass before the doctor sees the victim. But if the doctor will see him soon, give nothing to drink. In any case, don't give water if the person is unconscious or has an injury in the stomach region. Stimulants such as ammonia have no value in shock.

Don't disturb the injured person unnecessarily. Try to avoid measures that would cause more pain. Unnecessary handling and careless transportation make shock worse. It is best not to question the victim much or to discuss his injuries. Don't feed him. He should lie as quiet as possible.

These first aid measures—having the victim lie flat and providing the proper amount of covering—are very important. They help prevent shock; therefore, apply them at once. They also help if shock does develop.

A Scrapbook or Notebook for First Aid

Many students make a scrapbook while studying first aid. They usually make it in the form of a notebook into which they paste pictures and stories of real accidents and tell what the first aid should be. They draw cartoons and poster pictures, make rhymes, jingles, and safety slogans. They tell about conversations with people who had accidents or who often give first aid, for example, doctors, nurses, city policemen, firemen, highway patrolmen. Sometimes they write little plays, short stories, and radio scripts.

This textbook is divided into 17 parts or units. At the end of each unit are questions, problems, and things to do that will help you in making a scrapbook. You might divide it into 17 parts,

---

* This line in each unit marks the fulfillment point for minimum requirements toward Red Cross certification.

so that the material will be arranged well. A notebook with large-size paper is best. Use the loose-leaf kind if possible.

PROBLEMS AND THINGS TO DO

1. In case of an accident in your home when your parents are away, what neighbors might you call for help?

2. What is the telephone number of your family doctor? Of the police department? Of the fire department? Do you know how to call them?

3. In 1948 about a hundred thousand people were killed by accident. Name some cities that have about that many people.

4. In 1948 about 10 million persons were seriously injured in accidents. Name some states whose population is less than this. How does the number injured compare with the population of your state?

5. In Unit 1 you probably learned some new words that are often used by doctors and nurses. Make a list of them and of any other new words you learned. After each word write the meaning. If you are not sure of the pronunciation, look it up in a dictionary and write the pronunciation signs.

Did you know the meanings of all these words or expressions: immediate care, perspiration, unconscious, victim, vomit?

REVIEW QUESTIONS

(You might answer these questions in your scrapbook.)

1. What is meant by first aid?
2. Name some injuries that may cause shock.
3. By what signs can you tell that a person is in shock?
4. What would you do to prevent or decrease shock?
5. How do people sometimes harm a person in shock?

WOUNDS; DRESSINGS AND BANDAGES

WOUNDS

A wound is an injury in which the skin is cut or penetrated. For instance, a knife, bullet, ice pick, or wood splinter may inflict a wound. If the wound is deep, severe bleeding may occur, or there may be serious damage to structures within the body, such as the stomach, lungs, or brain.

In all wounds, even in small cuts or tiny stab wounds, there is danger that germs will grow in the wound, causing an infection.

What Are Germs?

Germs are tiny living things, so small that they cannot be seen except with a microscope. Many germs are helpful to man, but some cause harm. They are everywhere about us, in the soil and water, in our homes, on our clothes and bodies, and even in our mouths and noses. The skin is a strong protection against harmful germs, because germs usually cannot work their way through the skin unless it is damaged.

What Is an Infection?

Whenever we suffer a cut, germs are sure to enter the wound, being carried in with the object that cuts us, or being pushed in from our clothes or skin. If the germs grow in the wound and harm us, an infection of the wound is present.

The signs of a wound infection are these: The skin becomes red and tender around the wound, some swelling may occur, and

7

sometimes pus forms. These signs usually appear several days after the wound is received, though sometimes they occur within a shorter or a much longer time.

First Aid for Wounds in Which Bleeding Is Not Severe

The first aider should prevent more germs from entering the wound. Do not touch the wound or the skin near it with your fingers, with clothing, or with any other object. Do not breathe directly over the wound.

1. Apply over the wound a gauze dressing that is *sterile*—free from germs. Gauze dressings wrapped in paper and made sterile by heating can be purchased in drug stores. You must be careful when removing a dressing from its paper covering; wash your hands first and touch only a corner of the dressing when you apply it to the wound.

2. Apply a bandage over the dressing. This protects the wound still more and holds the dressing in place.

3. Send the victim to a doctor.

Sometimes sterile dressings are not at hand. In that case a clean cloth may be used. One can kill many of the germs on the cloth by scorching it with a flame or hot iron; or one may wash the cloth in clean water, or better yet, in soap and water, and then dry it. Sometimes, as on a hike, even these measures may not be possible. If so, the first aider can expose the cloth to the direct rays of the sun for at least 10 minutes. When a cloth is applied to the wound it should be folded to make several layers.

Every wound, even though it is the tiniest scratch, should be properly cared for, lest a dangerous infection develop. Sometimes, when the wound is very small, people do not go to a doctor but try to treat it themselves. There are several ways to treat a tiny wound. The family doctor can tell you what to do. Perhaps he will advise that an antiseptic of his choice be applied carefully to the wound and to the skin around it. Anti-

septics are preparations that kill germs. They also injure the body tissue somewhat; therefore, most doctors no longer use strong antiseptics on wounds. An increasing number of physicians advise that if people insist upon treating tiny wounds themselves, they should apply no antiseptic, but should wash the wound thoroughly in boiled or clean water, permitting no dirt to remain. A sterile dressing and bandage should be placed upon a wound after first aid. People sometimes apply lard, butter, oils, or even tobacco juice to wounds. Such materials should not be used. Do not put adhesive tape directly on a wound and do not use cotton as a dressing.

It is much better to go to a doctor than to treat wounds yourself, even if they seem unimportant. Many people have paid dearly in money and illness because they tried to save a dollar or two by treating injuries that seemed slight.

PRACTICAL WORK

(For study and demonstration)

Dressings (or compresses) are placed directly over wounds. Dressings should be sterile or as nearly sterile as possible. *Bandages* are used to hold dressings in place.

There are several kinds of bandages: triangular, necktie or cravat, and roller bandages. Adhesive tape is often used instead of bandages to hold dressings in place.

A triangular bandage may be made by cutting a strip of cloth, such as unbleached muslin, 40 inches square, diagonally. This gives two triangular bandages.

The parts of a triangular bandage are shown in the illustration.

A necktie or cravat bandage can be made from any fairly long strip of cloth. If a triangular bandage is folded over several times, it becomes a cravat bandage.

For use on small scratches, one can buy a strip of adhesive about an inch wide on which is a small dressing; this is a combination dressing and bandage.

When you remove a sterile dressing from its wrapper, you should be very careful not to touch any part of the dressing that will later touch the wound. Hold it by a corner when you remove

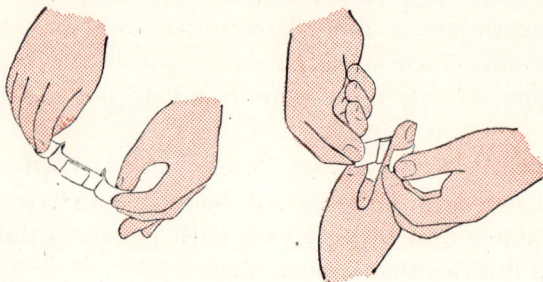

it from the wrapper and place it on the wound. Do not breathe upon the dressing. Why?

Roller bandages are frequently used by doctors; however, they are hard to keep in place unless tape is used, and will cause harm if applied tightly.

Class Work:

1. Examine samples of dressings (compresses).

2. Examine samples of bandages.

3. Show how to remove a dressing properly from its wrapping.

4. Show how to apply a dressing properly to a make-believe cut near the wrist.

DO YOU KNOW THE ANSWER ?

Question: John says that whenever he is cut, he never gets an infection. Why doesn't he?

Answer: He has been just lucky. The next time he gets a tiny scratch, it may be that a bad infection will develop if the scratch isn't properly cared for.

Question: Should you squeeze a pimple or a boil to get rid of the pus or water in it?

Answer: No. Even a small drop of pus contains thousands of germs. When you squeeze a boil to open it, you push many of the germs somewhat deeper into the body. Some of them may be squeezed into tiny blood vessels and carried deep into the body, where a dangerous infection may develop.

Question: What is the proper first aid for scraping wounds?

Answer: These wounds are called abrasions. The first aid is similar to that for other wounds. Dirt is often rubbed into the skin in these cases. Any wound containing dirt is likely to become infected. If the dirt remains permanently embedded in the skin it may act like a tattoo mark, causing a permanent scar.

A TRUE STORY

A boy, while bicycling, circled on both sides of a street and was struck by an automobile. His face scraped against the pavement. He applied a dressing but did not go to a doctor. Later his cheek showed a bad scar like numerous tattoo marks. Then, after several weeks, he went to a doctor who said tiny bits of dirt were embedded in the skin and could now be removed only if the skin were cut away. He said that some permanent scarring would result no matter what was done.

This story shows that it is best to get medical help at once after injury. The lifelong scar could have been prevented. First aid tells only what to do and what not to do until the doctor comes.

PROBLEMS AND THINGS TO DO

1. The following materials are used by some people on cuts, though their use is harmful: axle grease, tobacco juice, chicken fat, snake fat, body of a chicken. Do you know of other things put on wounds by people who haven't learned good first aid?

2. Cut out a newspaper story about a serious accident. How would you give first aid for shock to the victim?

3. Find out what size sterile dressings your parents have at home. What other first aid materials do they have on hand?

4. Write a short story about an accident you saw or heard about.

REVIEW QUESTIONS

1. What are germs?
2. What is an antiseptic?
3. Where are germs found?
4. What is an infection?
5. What is meant by a dressing or compress?
6. What is the proper first aid for a wound?
7. If you do not have a sterile dressing, what might you put on a wound instead?
8. How can you make unclean cloth safer to use on wounds?
9. What are signs of infection of a wound?

3

BRUISES;

THE CIRCULATORY SYSTEM

BRUISES

A bruise is caused by a blow to some part of the body that injures tiny blood vessels and body cells just under the skin. Usually the skin is not broken. When the blood oozes about under the skin it causes swelling and discoloration. You have probably seen the discolored skin near the eye of someone who has been struck there.

Cold, wet cloths, if applied immediately after the injury, help prevent the discoloration, keep down swelling, and relieve the pain. These cloths may be applied for a half hour, an hour, or even longer. If a bruise does not get first aid for several hours, warm wet cloths should be applied. If the skin is broken, give first aid as discussed for wounds.

THE BLOOD FLOW AND BLEEDING

In order to give good first aid to bleeding cases, you should have some knowledge about the main parts of the body and about the blood flow.

The body consists of the head, trunk, and upper and lower extremities or limbs. People often refer to the upper extremities as the arms. But in this course we shall use the word "arm" with the same meaning that doctors often give it—namely, as the part of the upper extremity between the shoulder and the elbow. Observe in the diagram the arm, forearm, thigh, and leg.

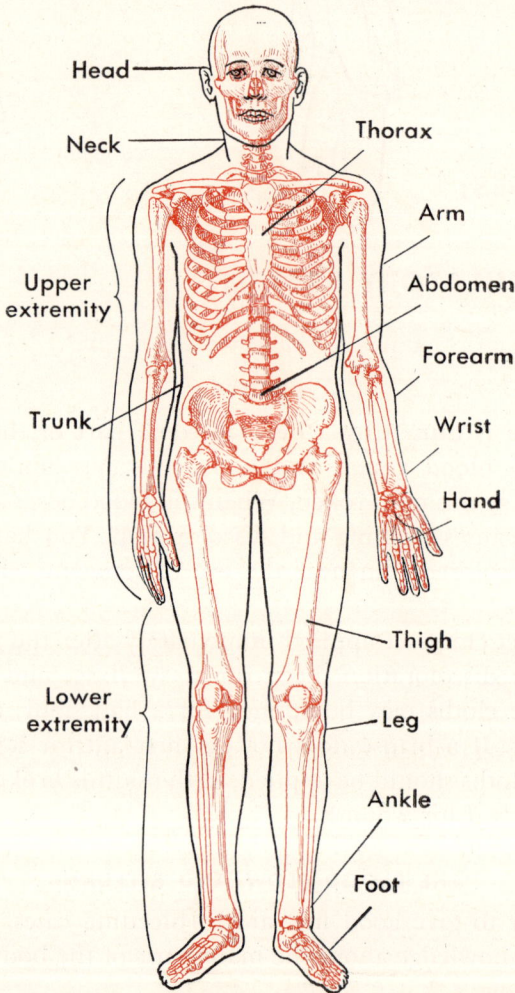

The Blood, Heart, and Blood Vessels*

An adult of average size has about 6 quarts of blood. The blood flows in tubes called blood vessels, being pumped along by the heart.

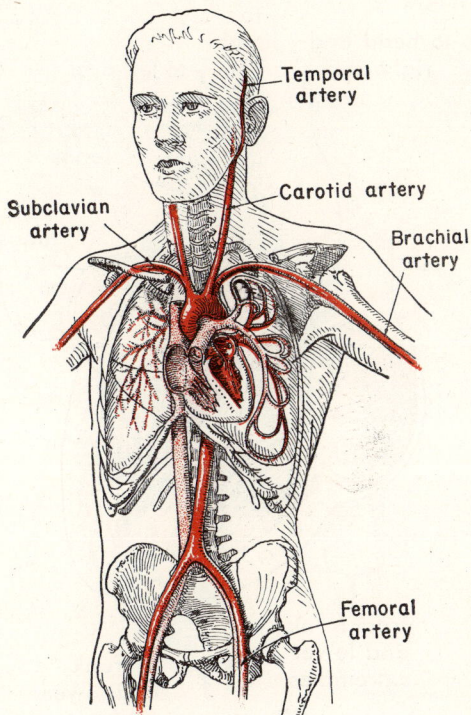

The blood vessels are of three kinds: arteries, capillaries, and veins. Arteries carry blood from the heart toward tiny blood vessels called capillaries. Veins carry blood from the capillaries toward the heart. When blood is pumped from the heart, it enters a large artery. The artery branches again and again to form smaller arteries. The smallest arteries lead to the tiny capillaries. Capillaries are very short and lead to veins. As the blood flows along, it enters larger and larger veins, which finally bring it back to the heart.

---

* Large first aid instruction charts showing the skeleton and main blood vessels can be obtained at nominal cost from local Red Cross chapters.

The heart has 4 compartments, 2 in the right half and 2 in the left. Blood in the right side of the heart is pumped into an artery and goes to the lungs. After passing through capillaries, it returns by veins to the left side of the heart. Then it is pumped

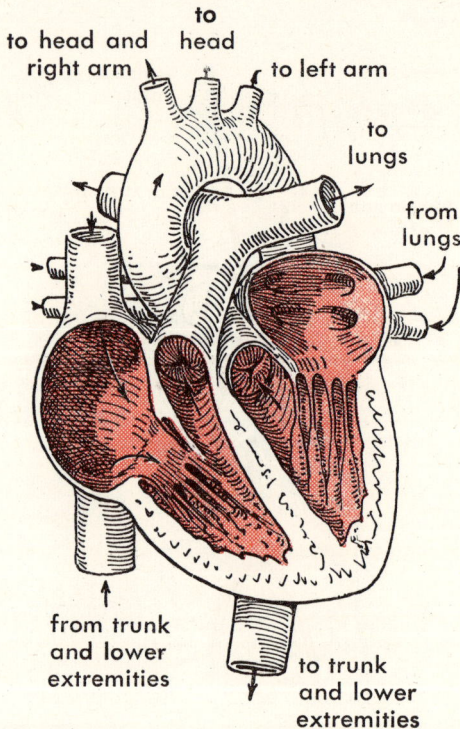

to head and right arm

to head

to left arm

to lungs

from lungs

from trunk and lower extremities

to trunk and lower extremities

into another artery and carried to all parts of the body. It returns by veins to the right side of the heart.

The heart consists largely of muscle tissue. The rate of heart beat in adults is about 65 to 75 times per minute when a person is at rest; but some people have rates as slow as 60, others as fast as 85. The rate is faster during activity and excitement. Children have faster rates than adults.

In most small cuts, only tiny capillaries are injured and the blood oozes forth. In larger wounds, veins or arteries may also be cut. Then the blood gushes freely or may spray up like a fountain. Blood from an artery sometimes comes in spurts and is brighter red than blood from a vein. But in actual first aid work it is very hard to tell whether an artery or a vein is bleeding; and it is not really necessary for you to know. *The important thing is to stop the bleeding at once.* You will learn how in the next lesson.

In the diagram, note the big arteries supplying blood to the upper extremities and to the lower extremities.

PRACTICAL WORK

Equipment needed: Triangular bandages, one for every student.

1. **Apply a triangular head bandage.**

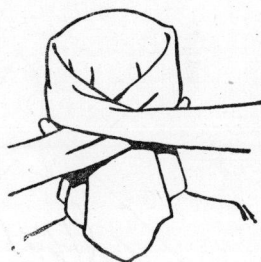

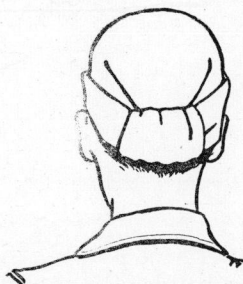

In case of a scalp wound, this head bandage may be applied after the dressing is in place. Fold a hem 1½ inches wide along the base of a triangular bandage. With the hem on the inside, place the bandage on the head so that the middle of the base presses against the forehead and the point hangs down the back. Carry the two ends around the head and cross (do not tie) them just below the bump at the back of the head. The top of the ears may be covered by the bandage if desired. Draw the ends snugly, carry them forward around the head, and tie in the center of the forehead. The point of the bandage, protruding downward in back, may be tucked in where the ends cross at the back of the head.

See how neat you can make this bandage. You should practice applying each bandage many times so that you will remember the steps. After your first attempt with each kind of bandage, apply a make-believe dressing before you practice putting on the bandage again. You can use a folded handkerchief or piece of paper as a make-believe dressing.

2. **Apply an open-hand bandage.**

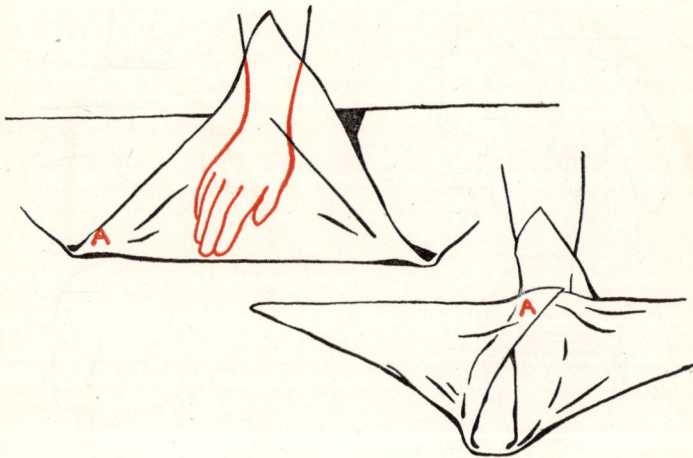

This bandage is useful in case of a large burn, cut, or mangling injury. First, place a dressing or a make-believe dressing over the injured area. Place the hand, injured side up, on the triangular bandage. Fold the point back over the wrist. Each edge is then folded inward. Now cross the ends of the bandage around the wrists as many times as necessary to make a neat bandage, and tie them together.

3. **The above bandage can also be used for a foot injury.** Try it, placing the foot on the triangular bandage so that the toes are directed toward the point of the bandage.

4. **Learn to tie a square knot.** If there is not enough time in class, try it after class hours. A square knot is very easy to tie, and should be used in first aid work.

Step 1: Place the two ends as shown in the illustration.

Step 2: Then carry end A down.

Step 3: Bring end B to the right, keeping it above the knot.

Step 4: Next carry end A above the knot.

Step 5: Then carry end A through the loop. Now tighten the knot.

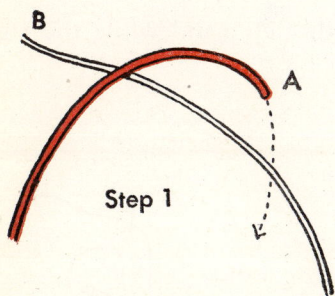

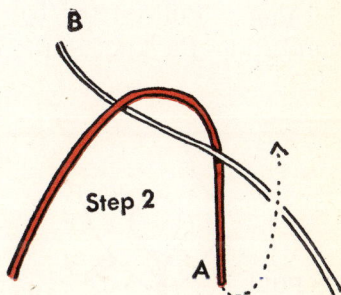

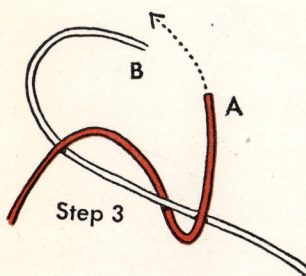

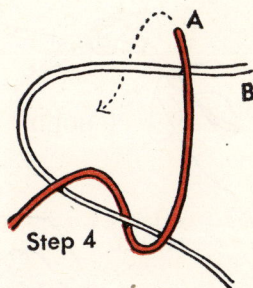

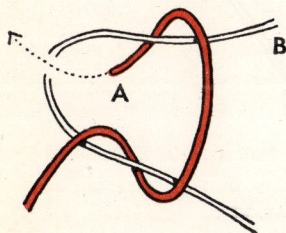

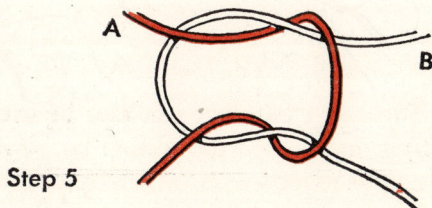

5. **Learn to untie a square knot.** This knot, properly applied, does not slip readily; yet it can be easily untied. One way to untie a square knot is shown in the illustration.

Step 1: Place both hands on the left side of the knot, the left hand grasping the band, the right hand grasping the end on that side.

Step 2: Bring the end over with the right hand as shown, *throwing the whole knot over.* Meanwhile, hold the band tightly with the left hand.

Step 3: Release the end and place the right hand on the side of the knot toward the left hand.

Step 4: Pull on the band with the left hand while the right hand slides the knot to the right.

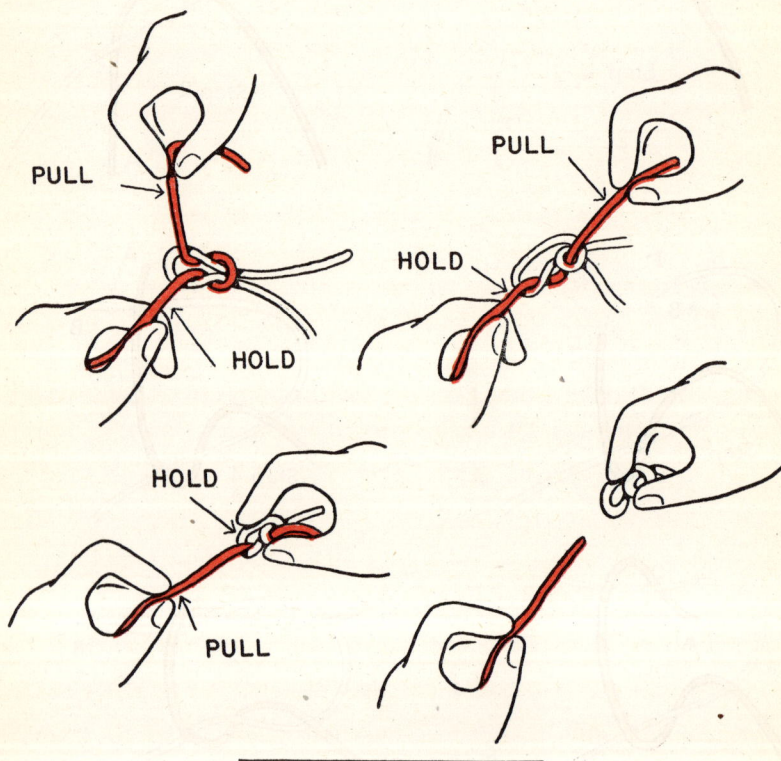

DO YOU KNOW THE ANSWER?

Question: John was struck near the eye by a baseball. He put a piece of raw beefsteak on the skin there. Was this good first aid?

Answer: Before people knew much about first aid they sometimes placed beefsteak on bruises. It is not a good method.

Question: How large is the heart?

Answer: Your heart is slightly larger than your fist.

Question: Is the blood always contained in the heart or blood vessels—arteries, capillaries, and veins—or is some of it in pools in the body, or just mixed with the flesh?

Answer: It is all in blood vessels or the heart. The same is true of the blood of fish, birds, reptiles, mammals, and some other animals.

Question: Are firemen and policemen required to know first aid?

Answer: In most large cities they must study and review first aid. In some small cities and villages they are not required at present to do so.

PROBLEMS AND THINGS TO DO

1. If you can obtain a daily newspaper printed in a large city, keep a record for a week or two of the number of accidents reported in it each day. Remember that although the newspaper story of an accident may be only a few lines long, there is often a long period of carelessness on someone's part before the accident. Can you make a story from this?

2. If you live on a farm or in a small town, make a list of accident cases you know about among people living near you.

3. Make some safety slogans. Here are examples:

> Look twice
> On streets with ice.

> Speed on the stairs
> May call for repairs.

You may be able to make some good drawings to go with your slogans.

4. Perhaps you can make some safety jingles. Here is an example from the National Safety Council:

> He's out of this world
> Is Ethelbert Flack—
> The streets were so slick
> And his driving *so* slack.

REVIEW QUESTIONS

1. What colors does bruised skin sometimes have a few days after injury?
2. What is the proper first aid for a bruise?
3. What is the arm? the forearm? the thigh? the leg?
4. Tell what happens to blood after it is pumped from the right side of the heart.
5. What is the important point to remember about first aid for bleeding?

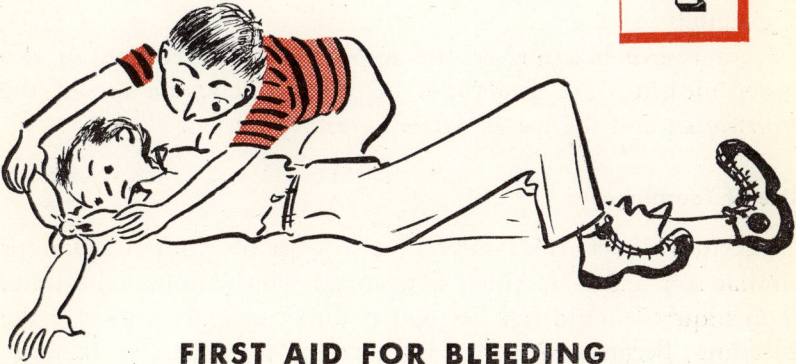

FIRST AID FOR BLEEDING

GENERAL FIRST AID MEASURES

Loss of a quart of blood by an adult or a proportionately smaller amount by a child is serious. This amount of blood can be lost within less than a minute if a large blood vessel is cut. Therefore, serious bleeding should be stopped *at once*. You do not have time to call a doctor first. You must give this lifesaving first aid yourself without wasting a second of time.

In most cases you can stop bleeding by putting pressure directly on the bleeding part. It would be best if you thrust a sterile dressing into the wound, but such material is usually not nearby. Therefore you must apply pressure with clothing or cloth at hand. This cloth should be folded to form a wad. It should be bandaged *tightly* against the wound. Do not remove it, lest bleeding recommence. If blood reddens the dressing, more dressing should be added.

Keep the bleeding person quiet. Do not excite him, or handle him roughly, or transport him carelessly, or talk to him unnecessarily.

If he will not soon be seen by a doctor, give him water, preferably warm, unless he is unconscious or has an injury in the stomach region. Treat him for shock and do not give him spirits of ammonia or other stimulants.

23

If a limb (extremity) is bleeding, raise it slightly above the rest of the body by placing blankets or some other object under the limb.

For severe bleeding of the upper or lower extremities two other measures are sometimes helpful—namely, the use of the *tourniquet* and the use of *finger pressure.*

Use of Tourniquet

A tourniquet (toor'-ni-ket) is a strip of cloth, rubber, or similar soft material, which is wrapped tightly around the limb. Tourniquets should not be used if direct pressure will stop the bleeding, because they may be harmful. A triangular bandage folded into necktie shape makes a good tourniquet. The band should be about 2 inches wide. A necktie, belt, or stocking can be used if better material is not available. Ropes, strings, wires, and very narrow strips of cloth do not make good tourniquets because they cut into the flesh and are painful.

For severe bleeding of an upper extremity the tourniquet is wrapped around the injured limb between the armpit and the elbow. For bleeding of a lower extremity the tourniquet is wrapped around the upper end of the thigh. Even though the cut is at the wrist or foot, the tourniquet should be applied at the upper end of the limb.

In all cases, after the tourniquet is in place, a dressing should be applied over the wound. If the injured person is not seen by the doctor soon after injury, the first aider should loosen the tourniquet for just a few seconds at intervals of about 15 minutes. If bleeding begins again, he should tighten it. If bleeding does not recommence, he should leave the tourniquet loosely in place. Tourniquets cannot be used in bleeding of the face, head, neck, or trunk of the body.

Use of Finger Pressure

Use of finger pressure at pressure points is often helpful in case of bleeding from an extremity. It takes time to obtain material for a tourniquet and to apply it. If bleeding from the upper limb is extreme, you can apply finger pressure on the inner side of the arm at the point shown in the illustration. For bleeding in a lower extremity, apply the pressure at the point shown. Apply the pressure in these places even though the wound is in the

lower part of the extremity. By applying this finger pressure, you prevent blood from going through the main vessel supplying the extremity because you press the vessel against the bone. Finger pressure in this way will not completely stop the bleeding but it will decrease it while you are getting a tourniquet ready, or while you apply a dressing firmly to the wound.

First Aid If You Have a Nosebleed

1. Sit up, holding the head tilted back very slightly.

2. Press the nostrils together, holding your pressure for several minutes.

3. Apply a large towel, wet with cold water, over the nose and face.

4. Do not talk, cough, laugh, walk about, or blow the nose. Activity and excitement may increase the bleeding or cause it to restart.

Summary of Important Things to Do for Bleeding

1. Apply direct pressure with a dressing or cloth to the wound.

2. Keep the patient quiet.

3. Use finger pressure or a tourniquet if necessary in case an extremity is bleeding severely.

PRACTICAL WORK

Equipment: Triangular bandages, sticks.

1. Practice applying a tourniquet. Fold a triangular bandage into necktie shape, 2 inches wide. Wrap it twice around the arm and tie a half knot. Place a short, stout stick over the half knot

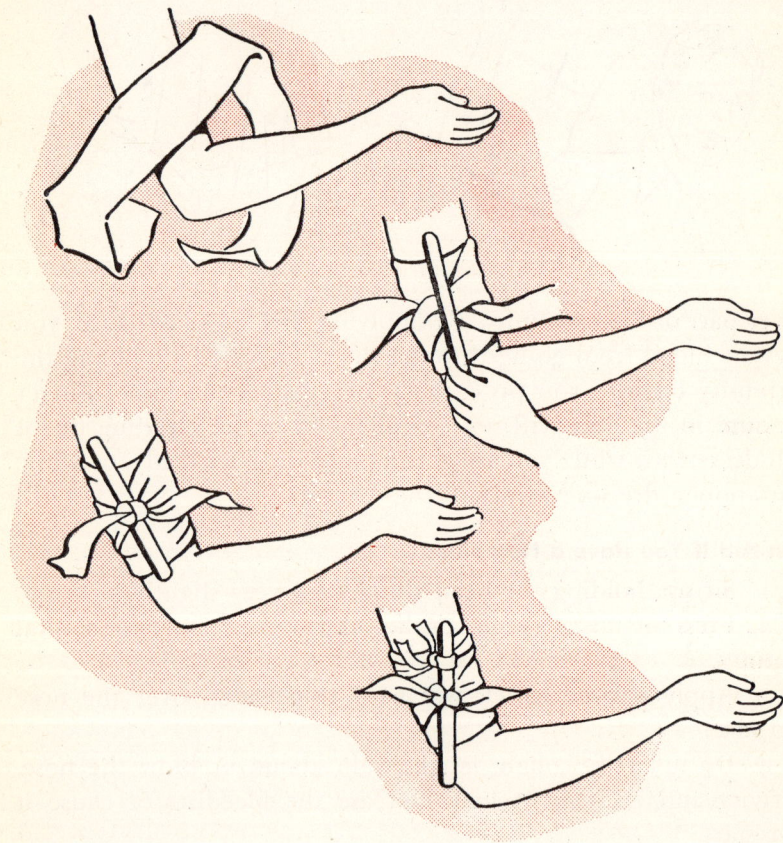

and then tie it securely in place. (Caution: a pencil or pen is not strong enough to use as a stick.) Twist the stick until it is somewhat tight and then secure it in place. In an actual case of bleeding, you must tighten the tourniquet strongly, but this should not be done in practice work.

2. Figure-eight bandage for the palm.

Lay the bandage on the wrist, with one end projecting about 12 inches beyond the wrist on the thumb side. Carry the other end around the palm, down to the wrist on the little finger side,

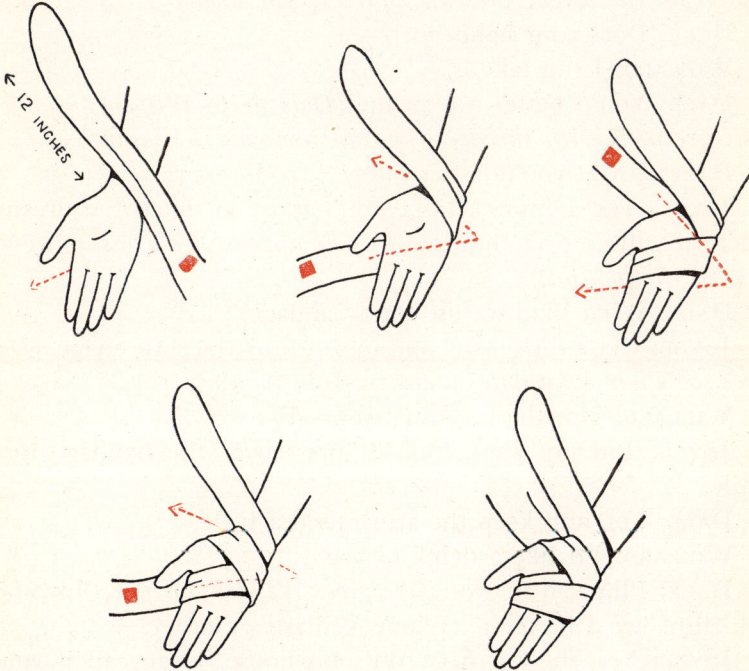

around the heel of the thumb, upward around the palm between thumb and index finger, and down to the wrist. Encircle the wrist, tying here on the side opposite the palm.

3. Stage a play.

CAST: *Three students: Willard, Joyce, and Dale.* SCENE: *A kitchen.*

EQUIPMENT: *A pencil (pretend that it is the knife used by Willard), a sterile dressing or a make-believe dressing wrapped in cloth or paper, a triangular bandage, a chair, a make-believe refrigerator.*

Willard, seated on the chair, is whittling on a piece of wood; the two other children are looking into the refrigerator.

WILLARD: Ouch! I cut myself.

(Joyce and Dale run to him. He is bleeding badly from a deep cut on the palm of the left hand.)

DALE: Joyce, get a dressing from the first aid kit in the hall.

(While Joyce is gone, Dale raises Willard's arm and presses tightly on the finger pressure point in the arm.)

DALE: Does your hand hurt?

WILLARD: I can take it.

DALE: You'd better not sit up. *(Dale helps Willard lie down. Joyce returns with the dressing and removes the wrapping.)*

DALE: Joyce, you'd better hurry.

JOYCE: Yes, I know. But I don't want to touch the dressing where it will go over the wound. *(She applies the dressing tightly against the wound.)*

DALE: What shall we use for a bandage?

JOYCE: Get a dish towel and fold it into a necktie shape. *(Dale does so. Then he applies a cravat palm bandage.)*

WILLARD: Has the bleeding stopped?

JOYCE: I'm not sure, but I'll press over the bandage for a while.

DALE: Yes, and keep the arm raised a little.

WILLARD: I'd like a drink of water.

DALE: I'll get it for you. *(He gives Willard a drink.)* Joyce, do you think we'd better telephone Willard's mother?

JOYCE: Yes, she's at Mrs. Wilson's house. I can call if you'll take care of Willard's hand.

DALE: All right, but first let's help him to the bedroom and cover him.

(End of play)

DO YOU KNOW THE ANSWER?

Question: What is usually the best way to stop bleeding of the scalp, cheeks, or forehead?

Answer: Direct pressure. Scalp bleeding causes a disagreeable sight. The hair becomes bloody and some of it gets into the wound.

Question: What is the most important way to stop bleeding from the neck and trunk?

Answer: Direct pressure.

PROBLEMS

Dictionary Practice

1. The expressions "a victim" and "a patient" are sometimes used to mean the same thing. Find out from the dictionary whether these words have the same meaning.

2. Many English words come from other languages, such as Greek, Latin, French, and German. Many of them come from the Anglo-Saxon, being used in Britain in olden times. Often the spelling and meaning of an English word today differ much from the spelling and meaning of the word as first used. The word *pupil,* for example, comes from the French word *pupille.* The French word comes from the Latin words *pupillus* (little boy) and *pupilla* (little girl). You see how the Latin meaning differs from the present-day English. *Pupillus* in Latin became *pupille* in French, and the French word became *pupil* in English. Most of the Latin and Greek words in the English language came to us by way of the French. When did the Norman French conquer Britain? Find from the dictionary the language from which *victim* and *patient* come.

3. Here is a list of words used in first aid. For each one write the pronunciation marks, especially the accent; the meaning that

the word had in Anglo-Saxon, French, Latin, or Greek; and the present meaning. You will need a good dictionary.

1. Accident	6. Doctor
2. Apex	7. Hemorrhage
3. Capillary	8. Infect
4. Conscious	9. Quiet
5. Cravat	10. Tourniquet

In future lessons you may wish to study new words in the same way and keep a record of them in your notebook.

REVIEW QUESTIONS

1. What is an artery?
2. What is a vein?
3. What are the different measures you can take if a limb is bleeding?
4. Why is the use of a tourniquet sometimes harmful? (Of course, occasionally it must be used.)
5. Suppose you apply direct pressure with a wad of cloth to a cut on the wrist, and then put on a bandage. If the bandage gradually becomes red, what should you do next?
6. Suppose someone on the playground is so badly cut on the leg that you know a tourniquet is needed at once. What can you use for a tourniquet?
7. What is a salve; how is *salve* pronounced?
8. A friend is badly cut at the wrist. Is it wise to let him look at the wound? If he needs a tourniquet, where would you apply it?

SPECIAL WOUNDS

AND EYE INJURIES

SPECIAL WOUNDS

Some kinds of wounds require extra care.

1. Wounds that may result in tetanus (lockjaw).

Tetanus (pronounced tet'a-nus) is a serious illness. The germs that cause this disease are found on farms, any place where horses are kept, or where land is fertilized with horse manure. The germs are often present in horse manure. They grow best in puncture wounds, which do not bleed freely. Therefore, wounds caused by nails, ice picks, sharp sticks or splinters, or any sharp object, especially if they are suffered on farms, are most dangerous. Tetanus may develop even in slight wounds. Powder burns, such as those caused by firecrackers, may also result in tetanus. For first aid:

    a. Encourage bleeding of the wound by squeezing at its edges.

    b. Apply dressing and bandage.

    c. Send the patient to a doctor.

Wounds like these, *even though slight,* should always be seen at once by a doctor. He can give an injection that prevents tetanus. Never wait to see if the disease does develop.

2. Wounds that may result in rabies (hydrophobia).

One of the most serious of all illnesses is rabies. It sometimes occurs following animal bite, particularly a dog bite. The dog *may* not seem sick. The first aid is as follows:

a. Wash the wound in water, for instance under a faucet (fô′set), but do not rub.

b. Apply antiseptic to the wound. A mild solution of iodine is a good antiseptic to use for this.

c. Apply a dressing and bandage.

d. *Send the victim to a doctor at once.*

If rabies develops, it always results in death, but the disease can be prevented if the injured person receives prompt care from a doctor. Only animals that have rabies germs in their mouths can spread the disease. But sometimes the dog does not seem sick at the time he bites. If the germs are developing in his body he will soon become sick and die within 2 weeks.

3. Snake bite.

Most snakes are not poisonous. For first aid in case of a bite by a nonpoisonous snake, one should merely apply a dressing and

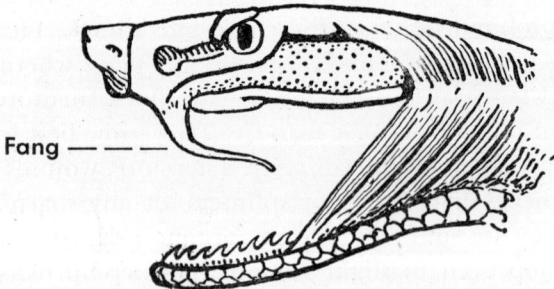

Fang — — —

bandage and go to a doctor. Certain snakes—rattlesnakes, coral snakes, moccasins, and copperheads—form poisons called venom, which they inject into victims when they bite. These wounds are

A. Coral snake.
B. Copperhead snake.
C. Rattlesnake.
D. Moccasin.
(Cottonmouth or water.)

usually inflicted on the lower or upper limbs. Bites by poisonous snakes require very speedy first aid.

a. Have the one who is bitten lie down at once and become quiet. If he runs away or tries to kill the snake, the poison spreads quickly through his body. *Immediate quiet* is very important.

b. Without waiting a second, the first aider should wrap a band tightly around the limb about an inch or two above the bite. This band may consist of a strip of cloth about 2 inches wide, a necktie, stocking, or similar material.

c. Then the first aider should make several cuts through the skin $\frac{1}{4}$ inch to $\frac{3}{8}$ inch deep. These cuts should be placed around the bite wound. If possible, sterilize the knife point first by applying a flame or by dipping it in antiseptic.

d. Next the first aider should suck on the wound. He can spit out the fluid sucked into his mouth; but if he swallows some, harm will not result because the poison is destroyed in the stomach. He should continue the sucking until the doctor comes, or while the victim is being taken to the doctor. The injured limb should be lower than the rest of the body, if possible.

If a bite is not located on a limb, a band cannot be applied, but all the other steps should be taken. In poisonous snake bite, then, think of:

(1) Quiet
(2) Tight band
(3) Cuts
(4) Suction
(5) Doctor

Very quick action in giving first aid is important.

4. Infected wounds.

If germs grow in a wound, the skin becomes red and tender. Pus may develop. These signs usually appear within a week, and indicate that the wound is infected. Never squeeze an infected wound. See a doctor. If delay in seeing him is necessary, keep the infected part quiet and raised on a pillow. Apply hot, wet cloths or towels, using boiled water containing 3 heaping tablespoonfuls of table salt per quart, or 6 of Epsom salts.

EYE INJURIES

Frequently a cinder or bit of dust lodges on the eye surface. Follow these directions to prevent trouble:

1. Do not rub either eye.

2. Never attempt to remove the material with a toothpick, match, or any other instrument.

3. Never examine the eye until you have washed your hands thoroughly.

Usually it is best to send the injured person to the doctor. If you are careful, you may succeed in removing a speck of material by using the following method:

a. Pull down the lower eyelid and see if the body lies on the under surface of the lid. If it does, it can be lifted off gently by touching it with the corner of a clean cloth.

b. Grasp the lashes of the upper eyelid gently between thumb and forefinger, have the patient look upward, and pull the upper eyelid forward and downward over the lower lid. If this measure does not help, do not persist in trying it.

Red eyes sometimes indicate that a bit of material has been present in the eye, or it may mean that an infection is present. In either case the junior first aider should not try to treat the eye.

If the surface of the eyeball is scratched, for instance, by a twig, or if an object such as a splinter enters the eyeball, even a small fraction of an inch, the injury may be serious. Even if you can see an object sticking in the wound, do not try to remove it. You might drag out some of the eye's precious contents. This injury is so serious that the injured person should be kept flat and moved on a stretcher. The sooner he gets expert care, the greater the chance of preventing serious trouble.

PRACTICAL WORK

Equipment: Triangular bandages.

1. Apply an arm sling.

The arm sling is useful in case of a serious injury to the arm or hand, because it gives good support. It is valuable also when the collarbone is broken.

Grasp the triangular bandage by one of the ends and hold it in front of the pretended victim so that the point or apex of the bandage is directed toward the elbow of the injured arm. (A simple rule to remember when applying an arm sling: Point the apex of the bandage toward the injured arm.)

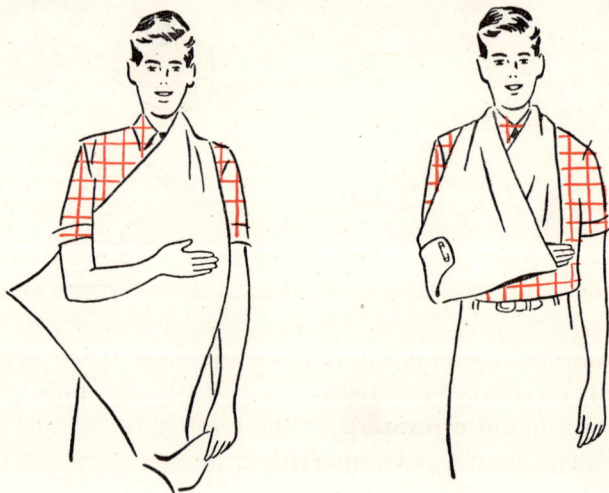

Then bring the lower end up over the arm and shoulder, and tie the two ends in back of the neck. Fasten the apex of the bandage with a safety pin or tuck it into the bandage. The sling should usually be so adjusted that the wrist is held several inches higher than the elbow. In an actual case, however, pain is a good guide.

Do not bend the elbow much if it causes pain. In fact, any procedure in first aid that causes increased pain is likely to be a
harmful one if a bone is broken.

2. **Apply a sling,** using a necktie, strip of cloth, or belt instead
of a triangular bandage.

3. **Apply a bandage between arm and wrist.** This bandage may
slip unless carefully applied, but it is very useful, because the
same kind of bandage can be used in case of injury *above the
elbow, above the knee,* or *below the knee.*

Fold the triangular bandage into a cravat. If the injury is
small, a cravat 2 inches wide is good; for larger injuries, wider
cravats are necessary.

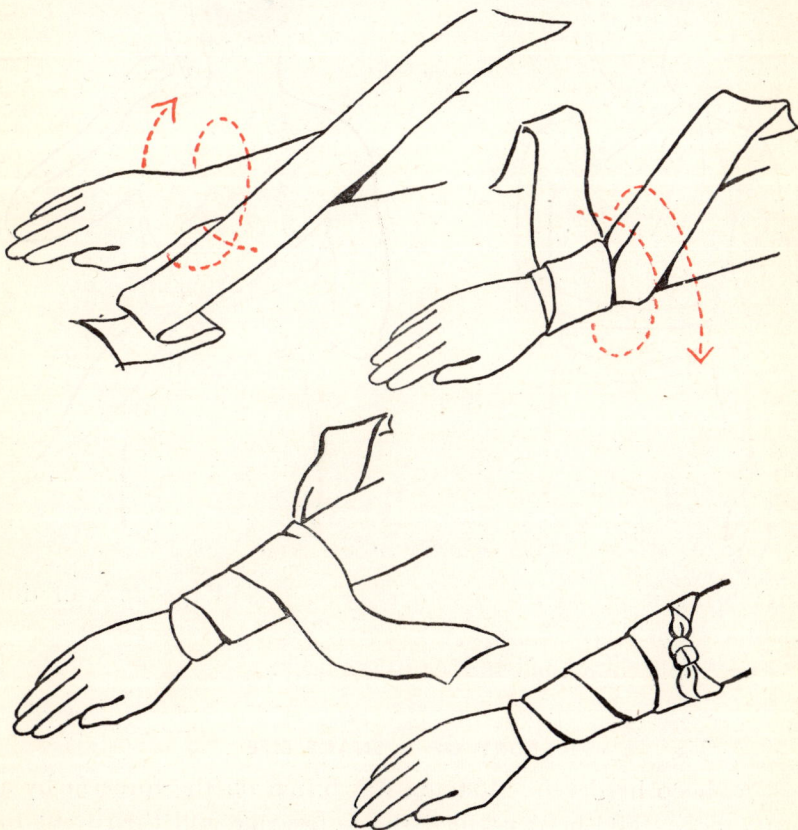

Place the cravat diagonally across the forearm, over the injury, as shown in the diagram. Hold the upper end steady while you spiral the lower end downward toward the wrist, and then upward toward the elbow. Tie the ends in a square knot.

4. **Apply a chest bandage.**

Place a triangular bandage against the chest so that the apex is at the shoulder. Have the pretended victim hold the apex there. Now fold the base inward as far up as you desire. Carry the ends around the body and tie directly below the shoulder. You will always have one protruding long end after you tie. Take this end

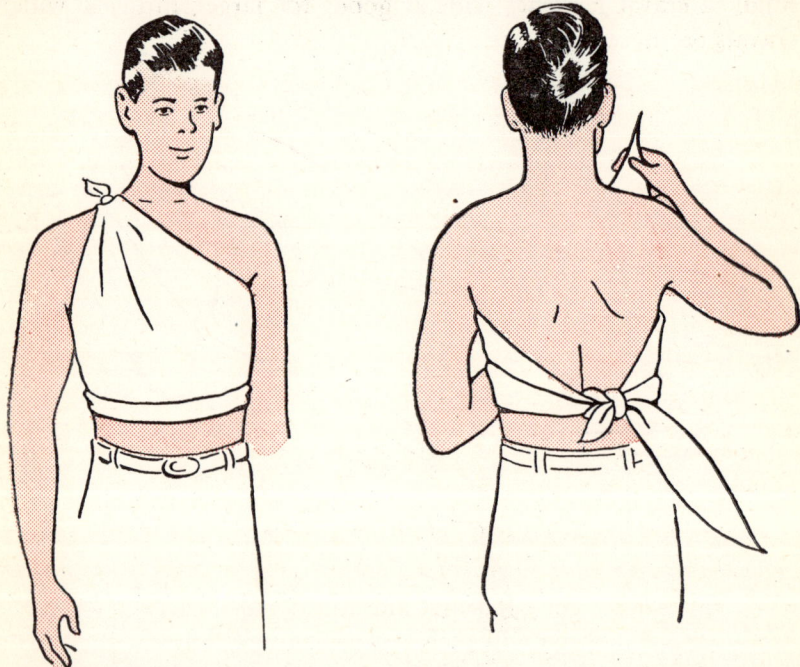

and bring it up to the shoulder, tying it and the apex of the bandage together.

5. **Apply the same bandage to the back.**

STORY OF A SNAKE BITE

A sheep herder in Montana was bitten on the forearm by a rattlesnake. The herder killed the rattlesnake and then went to his bed in the chuck wagon. There he made cuts about the bite and applied suction with his mouth. He was found dead the next day by a cowboy who was bringing a supply of food. What mistakes did the sheep herder make in giving himself first aid?

1. He spent precious time killing the rattlesnake when he should have started first aid immediately.

2. He did not become quiet at once. His activity in killing the snake caused his heart to pump harder, so that the blood carried snake venom more quickly to all parts of his body.

3. He did not apply a tight band above the snake bite.

QUESTIONS ABOUT TETANUS AND RABIES

Question: Why is tetanus sometimes called lockjaw?

Answer: The disease affects the nerves and, through them, the muscles. Sometimes the victim cannot control his jaw muscles well, and it may be rather difficult to move the lower jaw.

Question: Why are tetanus germs likely to grow in puncture wounds if they are carried there?

Answer: They grow best in wounds from which the air is shut off.

Question: Why is rabies sometimes called hydrophobia?

Answer: Hydrophobia comes from two Greek words meaning "water" and "fear." People and other animals who have rabies do not wish to drink, because they cannot swallow properly. They are not really afraid of water. Rabies is a better name to use.

Question: Do all people bitten by poisonous snakes die if they don't get good first aid and doctors' care?

Answer: No, some will recover even though untreated. But the chance of recovery is far greater if immediate first aid and medical care are given.

PROBLEMS AND THINGS TO DO

1. Young people are more likely to be bitten by dogs than are older people. If a dog bites someone, you may be bitten too if you try to catch the dog. Ask your teacher what should be done with the dog.

2. If you live on a farm, or know about farming, make a list of all the kinds of farm machinery that may cause cutting wounds.

3. Have someone in class ask a doctor about wounds he knows have led to tetanus. How was each wound caused? How big was each wound? Have the student make a report to the class.

4. Perhaps several class members will agree to ask someone who had an accident about the: (1) hospital expense; (2) doctor's expense; (3) cost of drugs, dressings, and so on; (4) loss of wages; (5) other expense. Have each of them make a report to the class. If possible, at least one case should deal with someone about your age.

5. Have someone bring to class pictures of poisonous snakes. Study the appearance of those found in your community.

6. Make a true-false examination dealing with the first 5 lessons. An example of a true-false question is this:

If a person is in shock, his skin usually is pale.   True   False

REVIEW QUESTIONS

1. Horses sometimes carry tetanus germs into cities. In what other ways may these germs be brought into urban communities?
2. With what wounds is there the greatest danger of tetanus?
3. What is the first aid for a puncture wound?
4. What is the first aid for a dog bite?
5. What is the first aid for a bite by a poisonous snake?
6. If a speck of dirt gets into one eye, should you rub the other one?

6

THE BREATHING SYSTEM; ARTIFICIAL RESPIRATION

The process of breathing air in and out is called respiration. If a person's breathing is stopped by an accident, the first aider may give him artificial respiration; that is, he causes air to enter and leave the victim's lungs. A junior course student can give artificial respiration just as well as an adult can. Giving artificial respiration to certain accident victims saves their lives.

Why Breathing Is Necessary

Oxygen, which is a part of the air, and food are carried by the blood to the body cells. There the food and oxygen unite, providing energy for our activities and heat to keep our bodies warm. The body quickly dies if it does not receive oxygen.

When food and oxygen unite, one product formed is a gas called *carbon dioxide*. Carbon dioxide has various uses, but because it is constantly forming, much of it must be thrown off. It is carried to the lungs and is expelled with the air we breathe out.

The Breathing Process

Air enters the nose and passes through the throat, windpipe, and bronchial tubes to the lungs. In the lungs the oxygen passes into the blood capillaries.

When at rest, adults breathe about 17 times a minute, children somewhat faster. About a pint of air is taken in and expelled

43

during an average breath. You can take in much more air than this in a deep breath.

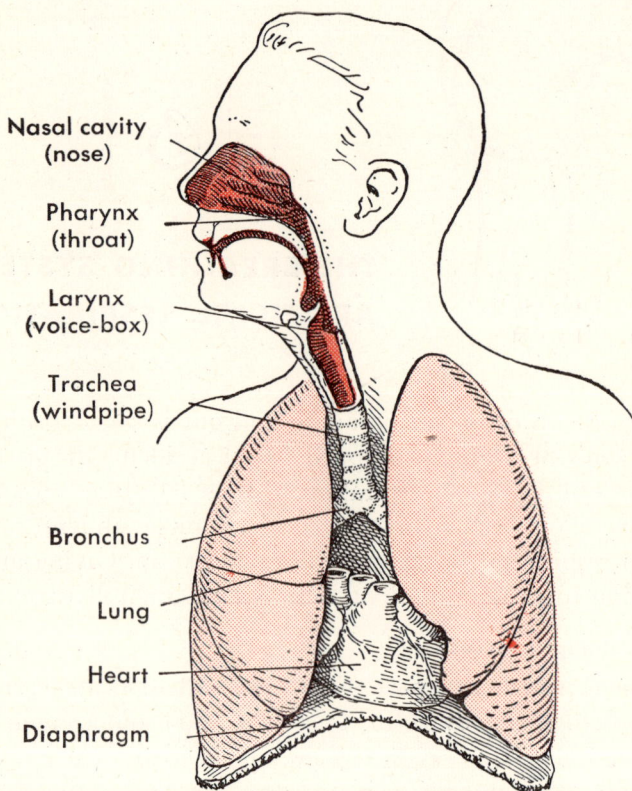

Nasal cavity (nose)

Pharynx (throat)

Larynx (voice-box)

Trachea (windpipe)

Bronchus

Lung

Heart

Diaphragm

Take a deep breath. Observe that certain muscles in the chest wall cause the chest to increase in size. Meanwhile, a muscle (the diaphragm) at the base of the chest presses down against the abdominal cavity. As a result the chest cavity becomes larger and air rushes into the lungs. Then the muscles cease their efforts, the chest cavity becomes smaller, and air is expelled.

The Way To Give Artificial Respiration

The Red Cross teaches the prone pressure method. It is called prone pressure because the victim lies prone, which is face down.

1. Lay the victim prone, with the arms placed as shown in the illustration.

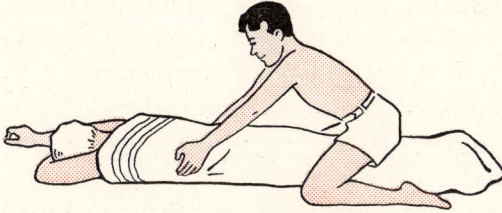

2. Kneel, straddling one or both of the victim's thighs. **Place** yourself so that, with your shoulders bent rather low, you can put your hands on the victim's back. The little fingers should touch the lowest ribs, and the finger tips should be just out of sight.

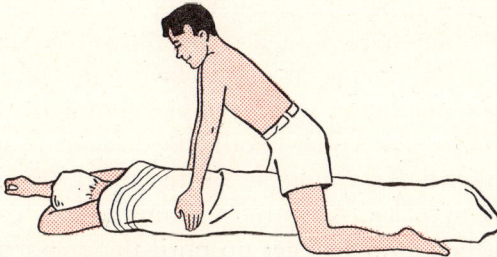

3. Swing your body forward slowly so that its weight is gradually brought to bear upon the patient. Do not bend your elbows. Do not go too far forward. At the end of the forward swing, your shoulders should be directly over your wrists.

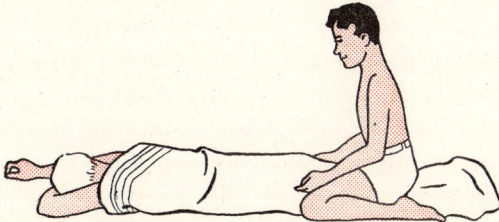

4. Now, immediately swing (do not push) backward until you rest upon your heels, at the same time bringing your arms back.

5. Then place your hands again and repeat the forward swing.

By pressing on the victim's chest in this way, you drive out some of the air from his body; and when you release your pressure, air enters his body. The double movement of swinging forward and back should take 4 or 5 seconds; therefore, the movements are repeated 12 to 15 times every minute.

Continue artificial respiration until the victim again breathes regularly of his own accord, or until the doctor comes and takes charge, or until you are *positive* that the victim is dead. The victim may start to breathe in less than 15 minutes. In some cases, especially after electrical shock, several hours of artificial respiration may be necessary. It is easy to tell when the victim starts to breathe. You can feel breathing movements and sometimes you can hear gasping sounds. Continue artificial respiration until the breathing is regular. Then watch the victim and be ready to start again, because he may stop breathing.

There are other important first aid measures. Have someone call a doctor or ambulance at once. Have someone put blankets under and over the victim while you are giving artificial respiration. The necktie and collar should be loosened, and someone should pull slightly for a moment on the tip of the tongue to be sure that it is in place. After the victim recovers consciousness, he should not be allowed to get up until the doctor permits.

PRACTICAL WORK

Equipment: Newspapers or blankets to throw on the floor.

1. **Practice giving artificial respiration** until you can give it smoothly at the proper rate. *Note to teacher:* A demonstration should precede this practice by the students.

2. **Practice rolling a person over quickly and gently.** It is important to *get started quickly* in giving artificial respiration to cases that need it. You should know how to roll a person over if he is lying on his back when you find him.

Supposing you are to the right of a victim who needs artificial respiration and who is lying on his back, try the following method.

With your left hand, grasp his nearer hand and extend it above his head so that it lies as shown in the illustration. Continue holding this hand.

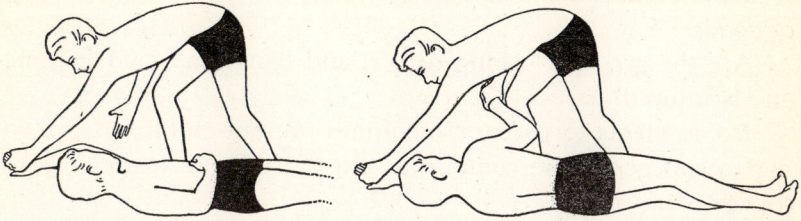

Quickly take his other hand and pull toward you so that the patient rolls over. As he rolls over, you can thrust his hand under his face so that he is placed properly for artificial respiration. Do this gently, lest you cause a dislocation at the shoulder.

Try the same method, working from the left side. Then quickly straddle one or both thighs and start artificial respiration.

PROBLEMS

1. Perhaps by this time you have collected a list of accidents that happened in your community.

The last war cost all of us much money. The full price will not be paid for many, many years. Another enemy, accidents, costs us much money. You become poorer even when someone else in your community is injured or killed.

In what ways does community tax money go to care for accident victims and their families?

How do accidents affect employment, wages, and production of goods?

Are the grocer, clothing dealer, and banker affected if someone is injured?

Do accidents to parents sometimes prevent children from going to college? Is the community hurt if a child does not get a college education?

How are you affected if someone in another family is injured?

You can easily see why everyone should help in the community fight against accidents.

2. Make a list of organizations in your community that *might* have a safety program. Do you belong to any of them? Do your parents belong to any? Does the organization have a safety program?

3. Make a list of a few people in your community who have been leaders in the fight against accidents. Perhaps you, too, will do more and more to help your community in this way.

REVIEW QUESTIONS

1. After air enters the nose, through what body parts does it go before it arrives in the lungs?
2. How fast does a person breathe when he is at rest?
3. How fast should we give artificial respiration?
4. How long should you continue giving artificial respiration?
5. Should you put blankets or coats about a person who is receiving artificial respiration?

7

ARTIFICIAL RESPIRATION AND RESCUES

When Does Artificial Respiration Help?

Artificial respiration may be required if:

1. The victim has been under water (drowning).

2. He has touched a live electric wire (electrical shock).

3. He has breathed carbon monoxide gas (usually from automobiles or other gasoline engines or from gas jets supplying manufactured—not natural—gas).

4. He has taken too many sleeping tablets.

5. He has been in a place where there was not enough oxygen—as in a well, cistern, or silo, especially during or soon after silo filling.

6. He has been buried by a cave-in.

7. He has choked on food or some object.

If a person has been in any of these accidents, give artificial respiration *provided* he is no longer breathing.

The best way to tell whether a person is breathing is to place your hands on his chest below the armpits at the level of the lowest ribs. If he is breathing, you can feel the movements easily.

Get Started Quickly

After a person stops breathing, his heart continues to beat for a short time. You must commence artificial respiration before his heart stops; otherwise it will be too late. Therefore, *get started quickly*.

RESCUING PEOPLE WHO NEED ARTIFICIAL RESPIRATION

In many cases when artificial respiration is needed, the victim must first be rescued, perhaps from drowning, from contact with

a live electric wire, or from a
gas-filled room. Many of these
rescues are dangerous unless the
rescuer has been specially trained.
Do not attempt a rescue unless
you are sure you will return alive.
Too many people are foolhardy
rather than brave; they impul-
sively try to rescue someone when
they have no reasonable chance
to do so; and then there are two
deaths instead of one. You have
a responsibility to help those in
distress if you can do it safely.
But common sense must be your
guide. You also have a responsi-
bility to your family, your friends, your community, and the
nation to remain alive. Many times you can aid best by obtaining adult help immediately.

Rescues in Case of Drowning

There is usually a safe way by which a junior course student
can help a drowning person. *But he should not swim out to rescue
anyone unless he has had life-saving training.* Even an adult should
not do this unless he is specially trained in making swimming
rescues.

Most drownings occur only a few feet from shore, from a dock or float, or from water of standing depth. If the victim is near enough, extend a pole, branch, or oar to him. Wade out from shore if necessary, but do not wade out too far. And do not wade out if the condition of the bottom is unknown, for a sudden drop-off, a hole, channel, snag, bed of quicksand or mud may cost your life as well as that of the victim.

> Don't make a swimming rescue
> Unless you are especially trained
> But you can help
> *Extend* a pole, branch, shirt or towel
> if the victim is within reach
> or
> *Push* or throw an object to which
> the victim can cling
> or
> *Throw* a ring buoy or heaving line
> or
> Row a boat and extend an
> oar to the victim

If you cannot extend an object to the victim, shove or throw to him something that will float. If possible, use a lifebuoy or a plank of oar size or larger. Smaller objects may help, but unfortunately most victims become panic-stricken, thrash about, and do not get as much benefit from a floating object as they might. Therefore, use a large object if possible. The victim should clasp it close to him and try to keep his face above water.

A good way to aid a drowning person is to use a boat if one is handy. The rescuer should know how to row and manage the boat. If waves are high or there is a swift current, or if the boat is small and unstable, no attempt at rescue by this means should be made because of the danger of being overturned.

The best way to approach a drowning person is to back the *stern* (or rear) of the boat within his reach and allow him to climb

in from there if he can, or to hold on while you row him to shore.
Don't allow him to climb in from the side. Sometimes the person
may be so far gone that he is in danger of going down before the
boat can be turned. In this case, row the boat alongside the victim
and push the blade of an oar within his grasp; then swing him
around to the stern and let him hang on.

Rescue in Case of Electric Shock

How electric shocks are received—A person while indoors may
receive an electric shock, perhaps fatal, by touching a bare electric
wire, a wire on which the covering is worn, or an electric socket,
especially if at the same time some part of his body touches a
grounded metal object—that is, an object that directly, or by an
extension, touches the ground. Examples of grounded objects are
radiators, kitchen sinks, bathtubs, and washbowls having pipes
extending to the basement or ground. A person may also receive
a shock if his body touches the part of an electrical apparatus
through which electrical current is flowing, especially if he also
touches a grounded object. Examples of such apparatus are many
kitchen appliances and the mechanism inside a radio. The dangers
are greater if the floor or one's body is wet.

Out of doors one may be electrocuted by touching an electric
wire or by flying a kite having a damp or metal string that touches
an electric wire. You don't need to touch a grounded object at
the same time, because your feet are touching the ground.

Rescue in case of electric shock in the home—Shut off the current if you can quickly do so. You can pull the main switch, or
you can grasp the electric cord where it is not bare or wet, and
pull it from the socket. At the same time avoid grounded objects.

If you cannot use either method,
try to remove the victim from contact with the wire by taking a *dry*
towel, sheet, or the like, encircling
the wire with it—don't touch the
wire—and pulling the wire from the
victim. Or—less safe—use the cloth to
pull the victim from the wire, being

careful not to touch him directly until his contact with the wire is broken. The wire may cling to him; therefore, you may have to pull his body some distance to break the contact.

In case of a bathroom injury it is probably best to turn off the main switch first or call the electric company. It is dangerous to rescue in a bathroom because there are so many grounded objects, the floor is often wet, and it may be difficult to remove the victim without touching him directly, especially if he is in a tub.

Rescue out of doors—Out of doors the danger in rescue is *very great*. The Red Cross recommends that you do not risk a rescue yourself; call the electric company or the police or fire department instead. But if you do try, use a long dry cloth, or a long dry stick—most sticks are not dry even though they seem to be—and try to move the wire from the victim. Remember that the Red Cross advises young people *not* to attempt this rescue.

Indoors or outdoors, after the victim is removed from contact with the wire, give artificial respiration if he is not breathing.

Rescue from a Room Containing Carbon Monoxide

Always open the doors and windows, or break the windows, to get ventilation before entering a room filled with harmful gas, if you wish to rescue a person. Otherwise you will be in danger from breathing the gas. There may also be danger that an explosion will occur. Stay some distance away from the room while it ventilates. This takes some time, but it is the only safe procedure for you.

In case the victim has breathed carbon monoxide in a small garage, the danger of explosion is much less. You can rescue him at once after opening the door if you can pull him out quickly while holding your breath.

PRACTICAL WORK

Equipment: Triangular bandages.

1. **Apply a cravat head bandage.** This bandage is useful for wounds of the forehead or scalp. Place the center of the cravat bandage over the compress covering the wound. Carry the ends

around to the opposite side of the head, cross them, and bring them back to the starting point and tie.

2. Apply the same bandage so that it covers one or both eyes.

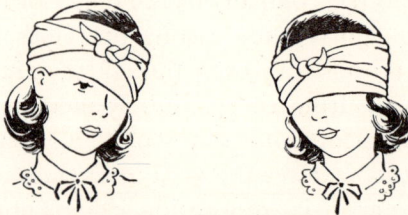

3. Apply a bandage over the elbow. Use a cravat at least 8 inches wide. Place the middle over the bent elbow, and carry the ends around, crossing them in the hollow. Carry the upper end entirely around the arm above the elbow. Carry the lower end entirely around the arm just below the elbow. Tie the ends snugly at the outside of the hollow of the elbow.

4. Apply the same bandage as above to the knee, but use a wider cravat.

DO YOU KNOW THE ANSWER?

Question: A man in a garage became unconscious from breathing carbon monoxide. After he was taken from the garage, he was still breathing. Did he need artificial respiration?

Answer: No, unless his breaths were exceedingly slow and weak.

Question: A boy riding a bicycle was hit by an automobile and struck his head on the pavement. He became unconscious and seemed to stop breathing. Should he have been given artificial respiration?

Answer: People who become unconscious following blows to the head in falls and automobile accidents usually have brain injuries. If they have stopped breathing, they are almost always beyond help. If you give artificial respiration by mistake to one who *is* breathing you may harm him seriously, for he may also have backbone or internal injuries. Therefore, in head injury cases it is probably best not to give artificial respiration.

PROBLEMS

1. Find where the main switch controlling electricity coming into your home is located and learn how to operate it safely.

2. Read the following discussion about water safety. Then decide how you can apply the safety rules. How can you help make your swimming place safer?

WATER SAFETY

Swimming is a great sport. It is clean and healthful. It develops many muscles, too. People who cannot swim miss all the fun at the pools and beaches. And they're not as safe as swimmers are when fishing or boating. Swimming is a sport in which girls are often as skillful as boys.

If you wish to learn how to swim well and how to float in the water, learn the right way when you begin. Have a good teacher help you so that you don't learn bad methods at first. The Red Cross has swimming classes in all parts of the country, taught by water safety instructors who are skilled in swimming and in handling small boats. Perhaps your physical education teacher or coach is a Red Cross water safety instructor. Find out from your Red Cross chapter or your teacher when and where classes meet.

Here are some helpful hints concerning water safety.

Swimming

1. Swim only in water that is known to be clean and safe. Swim by preference in swimming pools or at bathing places provided especially for people to swim safely under the supervision of lifeguards. If you must swim in a "swimming hole," be sure that there are no hidden dangers beneath the surface, such as dangerous currents, "holes" or "step-offs," or submerged rocks, stumps, or snags.

2. Never swim alone. Be sure that a good swimmer, capable of helping you in case of trouble, is nearby.

3. Swim only when you are feeling well and are warm and comfortable. Don't swim when you are tired, chilled, or overheated. Don't swim immediately after eating a meal, or in the middle of the day if the sun is hot, and don't swim at night at unlighted places.

4. While you are learning how to swim, stay in shallow water areas, where you can stand up at any time.

5. As you become a skilled swimmer, you may wish to venture farther into deep water. A good safety rule for swimmers is this: Swim only one-half as far out into deep water as you can swim. Then you are sure that you can get back.

6. For the most part you will want to do your swimming within a short distance of a dock, float, or beach. However, if you are a skilled swimmer and want to try a long swim, always have a skilled swimmer accompany you in a boat. He can help in case you get a cramp or become chilled and exhausted.

Boating

1. First learn how to float and to swim well. Then learn how to handle a boat before you take it into deep water. Perhaps your Red Cross chapter teaches boating.

2. You are not safe in a boat just because you can swim. When boating, you are often well beyond swimming distance from shore. Remember that wind, currents, and sudden storms may be very dangerous unless you have learned how to deal with them. You must therefore know how to handle the boat well and must know safety rules for boating.

3. Don't use a leaky or "tippy" boat, or pieces of board or poles in place of oars or paddles.

4. Don't overload a boat. A good rule is this: one person to a seat.

5. Don't stand in a boat. Sit on the seats in a boat and kneel or sit in the bottom of a canoe. Come ashore or into shallow water to change places.

6. An upset boat or canoe that is made of wood or a metal one that has air chambers will not sink even though it is filled with water. It will support you as well as a life preserver will. Staying with an upset boat until rescued is safer than leaving it and trying to swim ashore. Distances over water usually appear less than they are. Skilled swimmers have drowned because they underestimated the distance from an upset boat to shore. Remember, too, the effects of cramps and of clothes upon swimming.

Ice Skating and Ice Boating

If ice is 4 inches thick, it is safe even for groups of people. Remember that ice along shore may be thick, but over a current or farther out in a lake it may be thin. Ice that is honeycombed following thaws may be very unsafe.

REVIEW QUESTIONS

1. How can you tell whether a person is breathing?
2. Why must artificial respiration be started very soon after a person stops breathing?
3. For what cases besides drowning is artificial respiration sometimes required?
4. Tell what you can safely do to help a drowning person.
5. What should you do in case someone has touched a live electric wire?
6. What does *artificial* mean?

8

POISONING

Poisons harm the body when they enter it. Some materials are not harmful if eaten or drunk in proper amounts but are poisonous if taken in large quantity.

Examples of Poisons

Many medicines intended for application on the body's surface are poisonous if taken by mouth. Liniments and antiseptic solutions are examples. Medicines intended to be swallowed should be taken only in proper amounts. People have been poisoned by eating too many aspirin tablets, laxative pills, and other medicines.

Some cleaning solutions, such as lye, are very poisonous. Other substances that may be taken in poisonous amounts include kerosene, gasoline, alcohol, rat poison, ant poison, and poisons intended for spraying upon trees, potato plants, other useful plants and weeds, or for treating seeds. Frequently little children take these poisons without realizing the danger.

Some mushrooms (toadstools) are also very poisonous. It is extremely difficult to learn which mushrooms are the bad ones. The United States Department of Agriculture therefore warns

that wild mushrooms should not be eaten unless they are selected by experts.

There are many poisons besides those named here.

First Aid for Poisoning

A poisoning case requires quick first aid; otherwise the poison may spread through the entire body, or, in some cases, damage the stomach.

If you cannot get help immediately and you are sure that a poison has been taken, give the victim water to drink at once. This water should contain something that will cause vomiting. If ordinary baking soda is at hand, put 2 teaspoonfuls in each glass of water, and give several glassfuls, up to a half dozen if possible. If you do not have baking soda, use soapy water, milk, or even dishwater.

Meanwhile call or have someone else call the doctor and ask him what else to do. He will probably come immediately.

After you have given several glassfuls of liquid, especially if baking soda water was used, the victim will probably vomit. If not, try tickling the back of his throat or give him more fluid. After he vomits, give him some warm water and put him to bed while you wait for help.

In case of poisoning by acid or lye, do not cause vomiting. For acid poisoning, give baking soda in water, then milk. For lye poisoning, give much water containing, if you have it, lemon juice or vinegar, then milk.

REVIEW QUESTIONS

You probably know what a spelling bee is. Why not have a similar contest, using first aid questions? You can choose sides or arrange the contest in other ways. Here are some questions and problems for the contest.

1. Assign a bandage to one student from each side. Each student must apply the bandage. The one who does it best scores 1 point for his side. Examples of bandages are: open-head bandage, chest bandage, open-hand bandage, cravat bandage of palm, elbow bandage, arm sling.

2. Follow the same plan, doing artificial respiration instead.

3. Ask for meaning of perspiration, respiration, shock, dressing, bandage, sterile dressing, infected wound, antiseptic, cravat bandage, germ, artery, forearm, thigh, oxygen, bronchial tube, unconscious, victim. (Each word should count as a separate question.)

4. Ask these questions:

   a. Name three kinds of cases requiring artificial respiration.
   b. At what rate should artificial respiration be given?
   c. What is the proper first aid for a puncture wound?
   d. What is the proper first aid for a dog bite?
   e. What is the proper first aid for a bite by a poisonous snake?
   f. What is the way to stop bleeding of the scalp?
   g. Where should tourniquets be applied if they are necessary?
   h. What are signs of shock?
   i. What is the proper first aid for shock?
   j. What is the proper first aid for nosebleed?
   k. Name some materials that are poisonous if swallowed.
   l. What should you do in case of poisoning?
   m. When taking medicine, why should a person always read the label carefully?
   n. Why should people who have taken poison be given first aid at once?

9

BODY FRAMEWORK; FRACTURES

Broken bones are common injuries. By giving good first aid to a person who has a broken bone, you may lessen disability and expense, or perhaps even save his life.

SKELETON (BODY FRAMEWORK)

There are over 200 bones in the human body. These bones form the framework or skeleton of the body.

The Skull

The bony part of the head is called the *skull*. The skull consists of 22 bones. In adulthood these bones, with one exception, have grown tightly together. The exception is the lower jaw. The upper and back part of the skull encloses the brain. The lower front part forms the framework for the face.

The Spinal Column

The skull rests on top of the spinal column (backbone, spine). The spinal column consists of many separate bones. Within each separate bone is a hole. The spinal cord, a large nerve passing downward from the brain, is contained within these holes in the backbone.

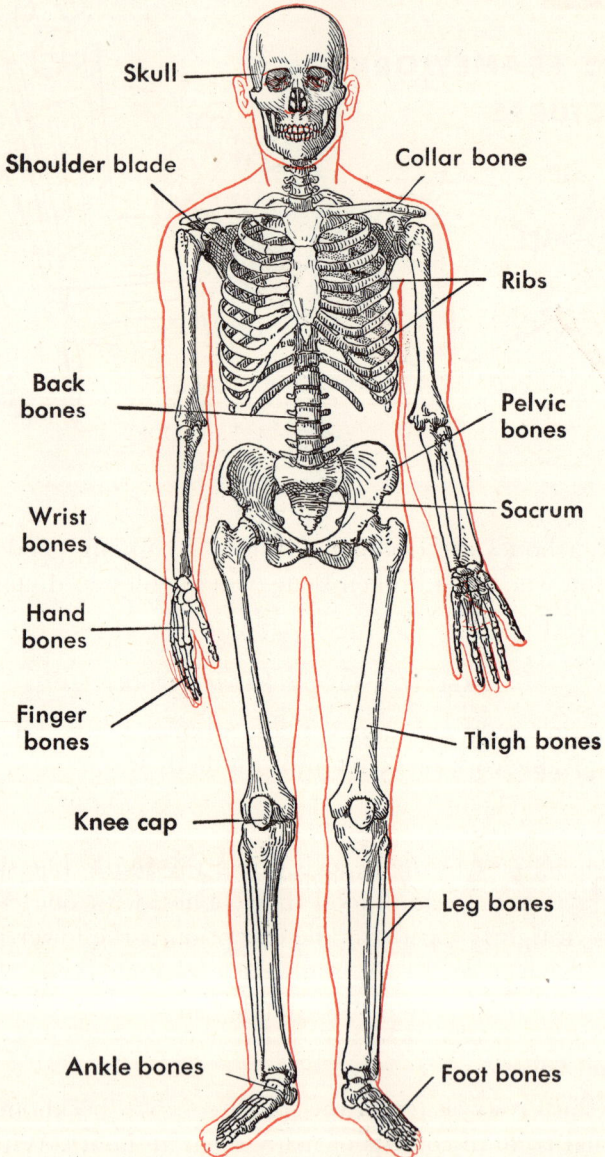

Skull

Shoulder blade

Collar bone

Ribs

Back bones

Pelvic bones

Sacrum

Wrist bones

Hand bones

Finger bones

Thigh bones

Knee cap

Leg bones

Ankle bones

Foot bones

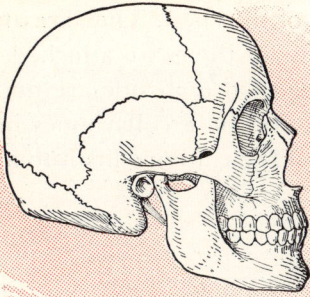

Skull—side view

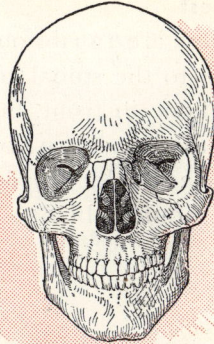

Skull—front view

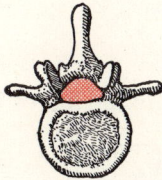

A vertebra

Spinal column

Side view   Relation to skull

The Chest

There are 12 ribs on each side of the chest. They are attached in back to the spinal column. Most of them are attached to the breast bone in front, but the lower 2 on each side are not.

At the upper part of the chest are the 2 collarbones in front and the 2 shoulder blades in back. The arm bone fits into a socket in the shoulder blade.

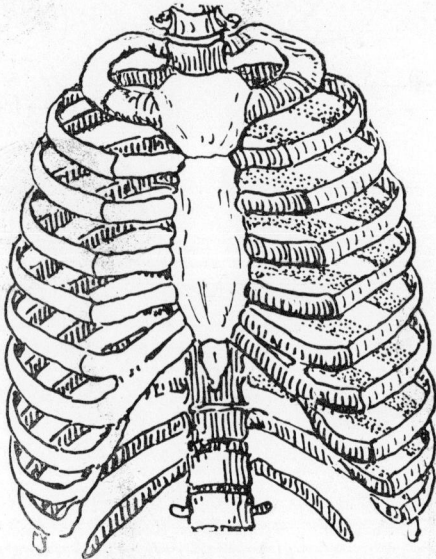

The Pelvis

In the lower part of the trunk a ring of bones forms the pelvis.

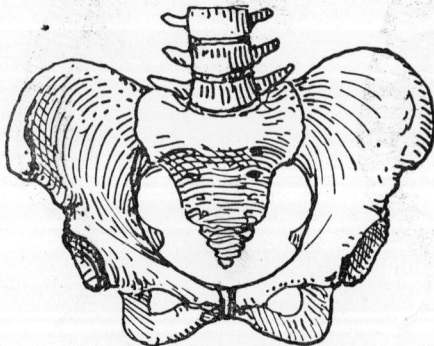

The Upper Extremities

The upper extremity has 1 bone above the elbow, 2 in the forearm, 8 in the wrist, 5 in the palm. Each finger has 3 bones, but the thumb has only 2.

The Lower Extremities

In the lower extremity there are 1 bone above the knee, 2 in the leg, and many in the feet. The kneecap is a bone located in front of the knee joint.

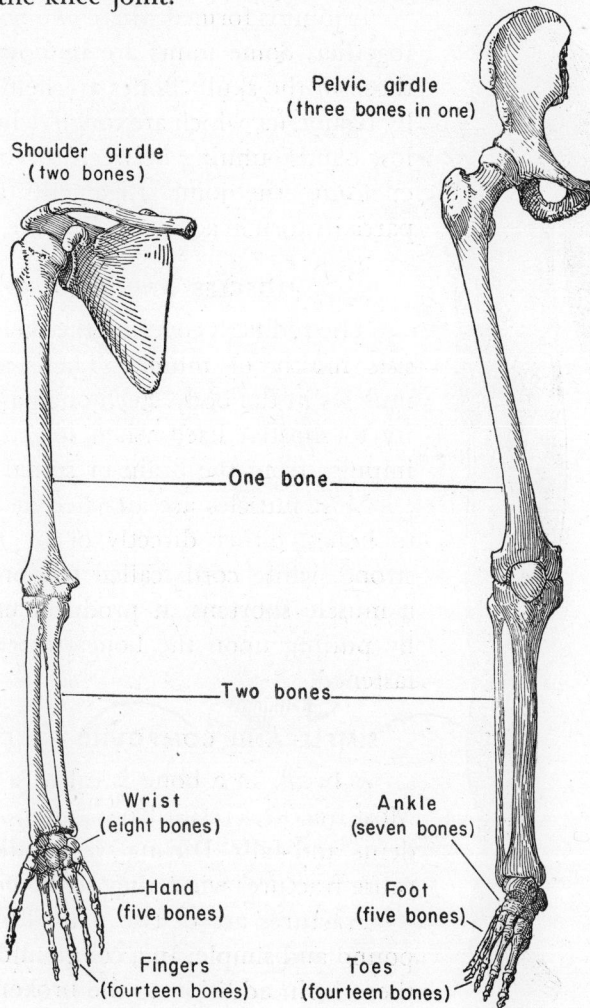

Pelvic girdle
(three bones in one)

Shoulder girdle
(two bones)

One bone

Two bones

Wrist
(eight bones)

Ankle
(seven bones)

Hand
(five bones)

Foot
(five bones)

Fingers
(fourteen bones)

Toes
(fourteen bones)

JOINTS AND LIGAMENTS

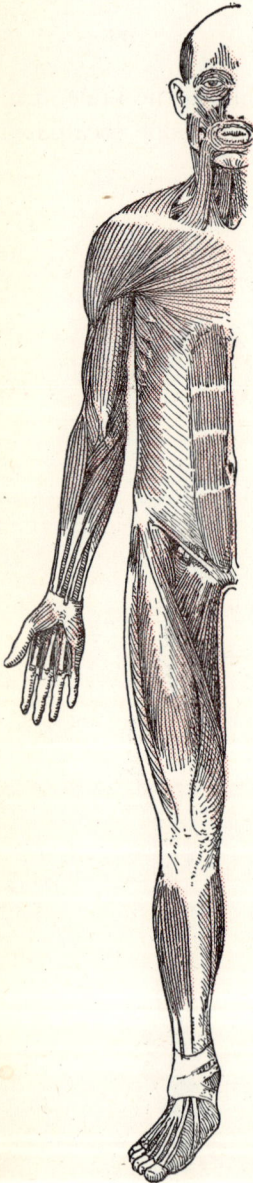

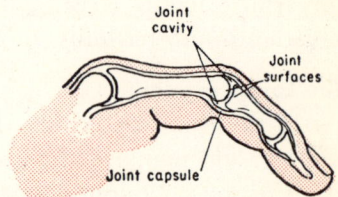

Joint
cavity

Joint
surfaces

Joint capsule

A joint is formed where two bones come together. Some joints are immovable, like those in the skull. Bones are held together by ligaments, which are tough, white or yellow bands running between the bones and enclosing the joint. Ligaments are often partially torn in accidents. They heal slowly.

MUSCLES AND TENDONS

The red flesh covering the skeleton consists mostly of muscle. There are many muscles in the body. Each one has the ability to shorten itself when it gets a nerve impulse from the brain or spinal cord.

Most muscles are attached at each end to bones, either directly or by means of strong, white cords called tendons. When a muscle shortens, it produces movement by pulling upon the bones to which it is fastened.

SIMPLE AND COMPOUND FRACTURES

A break in a bone is called a fracture. Most fractures result from automobile accidents and falls. During wars bullets often cause fractures when they strike bones.

Fractures are of two main kinds, compound and simple. In a compound fracture there is, in addition to the broken bone, a

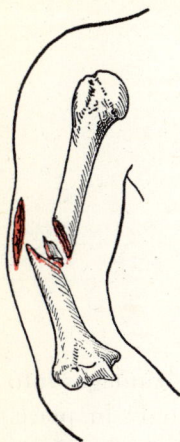

wound extending from the break through the skin. This wound may have been caused if a bullet or other object went through the skin and broke the bone; or the wound may have been caused if one of the bone ends protruded at least temporarily through the skin. In a simple fracture a wound extending through the skin is not present. Compound fractures are especially bad because germs are carried deep into the flesh around the broken ends, and an infection is likely to develop there. Simple fractures are bad enough, but with them an infection is much less likely.

If a person with a simple fracture is handled or transported without proper care, a broken end may pierce the skin. Thereby the simple fracture becomes a compound fracture. The same bad result may occur if a person with a broken leg tries to walk. A grave error in first aid is committed if a simple fracture is mishandled so that it becomes compound.

PRACTICAL WORK

Equipment needed: Splints, 3 x 17 inches and from ⅛ to ¼ inches thick; triangular bandages.

Junior course students should get help from adults in case of fractures. However, it is worth while for you to practice splinting for certain common fractures. Exceptional cases may occur where you may have to rely upon yourself.

Splints should be wrapped in cloth, especially if they are made of rough wood.

1. Apply splints for a fracture of the forearm.

This fracture is very common. Many boys and girls have suffered the injury because of falls when ice skating, when climbing trees or ladders, or in many other ways. Often the break is in the lower part of the forearm, and the victim thinks that the injury is a sprain of the wrist.

It is best to use 2 splints. One should extend from the elbow to the fingers on the palm side, and the other splint should be

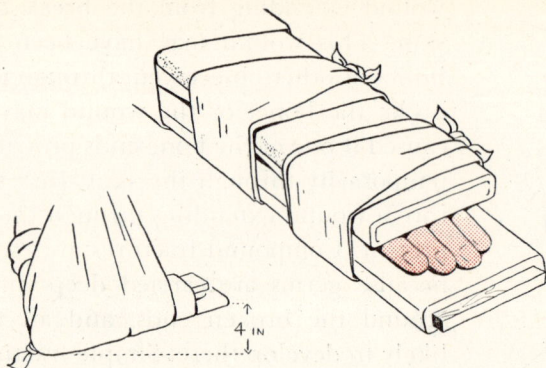

placed on the opposite side. Fold several triangular bandages into cravat shape, and use them to bind the splints snugly in place. Three or 4 bandages are usually required, though two will do fairly well if more bandages cannot be found. Handle the arm very gently when applying the splints.

After the splint is applied, put on an arm sling to support the injured extremity.

2. **Apply a splint for a fracture in the palm or at the wrist.**

In case of a palm or wrist injury, one splint is sufficient. It should extend from below the elbow to the finger tips. Place it on the palm side and bandage securely in place. Then put on an arm sling.

DO YOU KNOW THE ANSWER?

Question: Should an injured person be given a drink of whiskey as a first aid measure?

Answer: The Red Cross does not advise the giving of alcoholic drinks as first aid.

Question: Is it true that drunken people are very seldom injured in accidents?

Answer: No. Drunken people are more often involved in accidents than others. They are *more* likely to be killed or injured in accidents than others are.

PROBLEMS

1. Make drawings of several parts of the skeleton.

2. Make a fairly large drawing of your hand, showing the thumb side. Can you feel just where the joints in your index finger are? In your drawing you might show the bones in the index finger.

3. First aid is taught in many places. Sometimes records of the effects of first aid teaching are kept. From these records it appears that people who have studied the subject give better first aid to the injured than others do. They also *have fewer accidents* themselves after they study the course. Why do you suppose first aid teaching causes class members to have fewer accidents in later life?

REVIEW QUESTIONS

1. What is meant by *fractured bone?*
2. What is a compound fracture?
3. Why is a compound fracture usually more serious than simple fracture of the same bone?
4. How could improper first aid cause a simple fracture to become a compound fracture?
5. What is meant by skeleton, skull, spinal column, collarbone, shoulder blade, upper extremity, kneecap, joint, ligament?

10

SIGNS OF AND FIRST AID FOR FRACTURES

Signs of a Fracture

In case of a fall, blow, gunshot wound, or automobile accident, the victim may suffer a fracture. These are signs sometimes found when a fracture is present:

1. *Pain.* At the moment of injury, fractures usually cause pain, but sometimes the victim is so excited or afraid that he does not feel hurt. Later on, pain may be so slight that the victim sometimes thinks he has only a bruise or a sprain. However, if he moves the injured part, he usually has pain.

2. *Tenderness.* The skin overlying a fracture is tender, that is, it hurts when touched.

3. *Lack of motion.* The victim usually does not wish to move the injured part. He senses that pain will result from motion. However, he can sometimes move nearby parts rather freely. For instance, often a patient will move his fingers somewhat freely even though a fracture near the wrist is present.

4. *Swelling.* Swelling usually develops soon around the injured part if a fracture is present.

5. *Deformity.* The body part that is injured may seem deformed, that is, out of shape.

6. *Discoloration.* Sometimes the skin overlying the fracture becomes red or purple. We say, therefore, that it is discolored.

Common signs of fracture, then, are pain, tenderness, lack of motion, swelling, deformity, and discoloration. Often *only one or two* of these signs may be present, even though the victim has a fracture. It is wise to play safe by obtaining medical attention when there is any possibility that a fracture is present. If the victim does not receive prompt care, serious harm may result.

First Aid for Fractures

When bones are broken, a good rule to follow is this: *Do not permit motion of the broken ends or of the joints near the injury.*

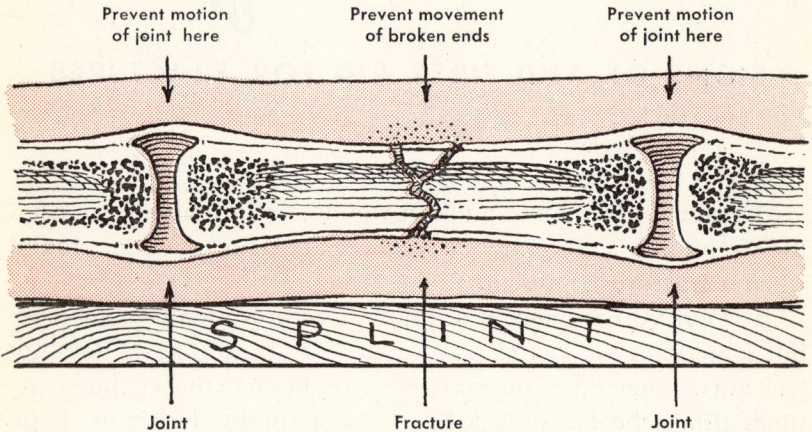

Prevent motion of joint here   Prevent movement of broken ends   Prevent motion of joint here

Joint   Fracture   Joint

If the ends move in the flesh, they damage the flesh, blood vessels, and nerves. If there is motion at the nearby joints, the broken bone ends move also. By splinting a limb and using arm slings and stretchers, the broken bone ends and the nearby joints are kept motionless. Unless the victim lies in a place where there is extreme, immediate danger to his life, his fracture should always be protected by splints or in other ways before he is moved even a short distance.

What to do—Although a junior course first aider should usually not splint or transport a seriously injured person, he can help the fracture victim very much if he is careful. He should take time to follow the right methods, because haste is unnecessary and often harmful in fracture cases. Too many victims are greatly injured because they are rushed away improperly.

1. The victim should lie down. If the injury is in a lower limb, he should not first try to stand or walk.

2. He should be properly covered. In warm weather he needs

only light covering. He should also have a blanket or coat beneath him. Unless the first aider is extremely careful, harm may result when the blanket or coat is placed beneath the victim. The danger is greatest in case of fracture of the back, thigh bone, or leg. If there is danger of harming, the procedure should be followed only when help will not come for many minutes or if the weather is very cold.

3. If a parent, teacher, physician, or any adult who is likely to know what to do is nearby, tell him to come at once. But if a telephone call or a trip of some length is necessary to summon help, it is best to learn something first about the injuries.

4. If you must examine the victim, first ask him where his injuries seem to be. Look carefully at the part that appears to be injured. Perhaps you can see it easily. Is there swelling or deformity? Is there a wound? Sometimes the injured part is hidden by clothing. If you can expose the injured part easily by turning back a sleeve or trouser leg or by unbuttoning the shirt, you may do this. But be careful not to injure the victim when you try to see what is wrong. You can easily harm him in your attempts to remove clothing or to turn it aside. For example, in case of a fractured ankle, if you try to take off the shoe you may cause much added injury and pain. If necessary, touch the possibly injured part through the clothing. In this way you find whether the part is tender or deformed. Even though you do not learn exactly what is wrong, you can find what body part is injured. Then when you telephone or send a message, you can give this information.

5. While help is coming, cheer the person if he is in distress. But do not talk too much to him, excite him, cause him pain, or disturb him unnecessarily by long examination.

6. Sometimes in case of a compound fracture, serious bleeding occurs. You should stop the bleeding by applying pressure. In rare cases, a tourniquet may be necessary. If a broken bone is sticking through the skin, do not push it back. If help will not soon be at hand, put a dressing, preferably sterile, on compound fracture wounds, and bandage it in place.

Sometimes an injury occurs when help is far away. In cases like this, the first aider must consider the seriousness of the injury, the amount of covering he has for the victim, and the weather. With really serious injuries, it is best, even in cold weather, rain, or snow, to let the victim lie quietly while help is summoned. The injured person should be well covered, of course; coats for covering him are usually at hand. With very mild injuries of the ribs, forearm, or hand, it is sometimes safe to transport the victim to help or assist him in getting there. If a mild injury of the ankle or foot is present, there is the possibility of fracture; therefore, walking may be harmful.

PRACTICAL WORK

Equipment: Splints, 3 x 17 x 1/8 to 1/4 inches; triangular bandages; blanket or pillow.

1. **Give first aid for a fracture at the ankle.**

It is often difficult to tell whether an ankle injury is a sprain or a fracture. Fractures usually give more pain and cause more swelling. But sometimes they don't pain much and don't result in much swelling. When you are in doubt, handle the case as you would a fracture.

There are several good ways to give first aid for a fracture at the ankle, if you must rely on yourself. The victim should always lie down. If he must be transported, use a stretcher. Stretchers are discussed in Unit 13. You should also use a pillow, blanket, or similar object to keep the broken ends quiet, or you can apply two splints.

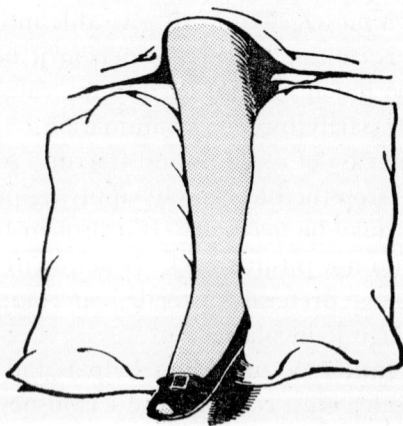

The illustration shows how a pillow can be used.

If you use splints, it is best to put padding around the ankle first. The splints should be placed on each side, and should extend from the heel to a point an inch or two below the knee.

Practice these methods.

(If the injury is just above the ankle, even a half inch, the bone may be broken entirely through, and the case should be treated as described in 3 below.)

2. Give first aid for a crushed foot or a fracture in the foot or toe.

It is best to support the foot on a pillow or on a blanket, coat, or similar object folded into pillow shape. No wood splint need be used. It is usually not necessary to wrap the pillow around the foot. If you do wrap the pillow or blanket around the foot and apply a bandage, keep this support fairly loose.

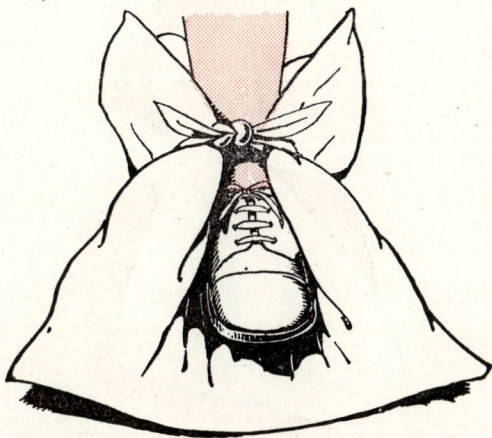

3. Give first aid for a fractured leg.

This is the part between the knee and the ankle. The injury is so serious that you should wait for help. You can place a pillow or a folded coat or blanket against each side of the injured leg. In this way you help keep the broken ends quiet. Be sure to give first aid for shock. A physician might splint a fractured leg by wrapping a pillow about it if the break is just above the ankle, or by applying splints to each side of the extremity from the heel to the upper end of the thigh, or better yet by applying a special device called a traction splint.

4. Give first aid for a broken collarbone.

This bone can easily be felt. Run your hand along the collarbone. For first aid, splints are not used. An arm sling is applied to support the upper extremity on the side on which the collarbone is broken.

DO YOU KNOW THE ANSWER?

Question: A boy fell from a tree, hurting his right forearm just above the wrist. He gave the injury no care but went to school and did some work. The next day the swelling was worse. He went to a doctor who said the forearm was fractured. Does it happen often that people with fractures do not get care at once?

Answer: It happens rather often that people think an injury is only a bump, bruise, or sprain, even though it is a fracture, and they wait a day or more before going to a doctor. Some people with fractures of the thigh or leg are foolish enough to try standing up. If people with fractures wait before getting a doctor's care, *serious* harm is much more likely.

PROBLEMS

1. Make a list of things you *have done* to prevent accidents in your home since you started to study first aid.

2. Icy steps and sidewalks often cause accidents. One boy decided that he would remove the ice near his home. In another home a girl planned a good place to put poisons so that her little sister could not reach them. One girl convinced her father that he should paint the basement steps white and should put in an electric light near the steps. Make a list of things you *can do* to make your home, farm, or school safer.

REVIEW QUESTIONS

1. List common causes of falls in or around the home, farm, school.
2. What are the signs of a fracture?
3. Might a person have a fracture if only one or two of these signs are present?
4. What is meant by *deformed*?
5. A boy injured his forearm. When he touched the injured part, he had pain. After a while he noticed some swelling. He could move his fingers easily. Might this be a fracture?
6. What is a good rule to follow in giving first aid to a fracture victim?
7. List in order what you should do in case someone seems to have a fracture.
8. Should you give first aid for shock in case of a fracture?

DISLOCATIONS AND SPRAINS

DISLOCATIONS

Because of a fall or blow, a bone may be dislocated, that is, sprung out of place at a joint. The signs are almost like those for a fracture. One usually cannot tell except by X-ray whether a bone is dislocated or broken. You should therefore give first aid in the same way as already described for a fracture.

SPRAINS

Sprains sometimes occur when there is great pressure on the bones and surrounding flesh at a joint. For instance, when a person twists his foot, he puts much strain on the ankle joint. In case of sprain the bone does not spring out of place or break, but the flesh around the joint (ligaments, muscles, and tendons) is stretched or even torn somewhat.

Pain is present at first, then swelling and perhaps discoloration. The commonest sprains occur at the ankle and wrist.

Since one cannot be sure whether the injury is a sprain or a fracture, X-ray is always advisable. Sometimes people with ankle fractures are wrongly permitted to walk because the first aider thinks the injury is a sprain. Even in sprain cases it is best not to walk until the doctor advises it.

Cloths wet with cold water should be applied to a sprain, the sooner after injury the better. Cold cloths do not have nearly so much value if their application is delayed even 15 minutes. The cold applications may be continued a half hour or longer. The injured part should be kept quiet. It is best that the victim lie down with the injured part elevated somewhat on a pillow or other support. The doctor may advise that warm applications be applied later on, or he may tape the ankle.

PRACTICAL WORK*

1. Send someone to the front of the class. Have him point to different parts of his body. Each time he does so, tell how to stop bleeding in case of a cut in that part of the body.

2. Have a review practice in giving artificial respiration.

3. Have a review practice in applying the bandages you have learned, and in tying square knots.

QUESTIONS AND ANSWERS

Question: A highway patrolman finds that a victim of an automobile accident has a severe backache. The patrolman fears that there is a fracture of one of the bones in the spinal column. What is the proper first aid?

Answer: It would be safest to have a doctor come. Fractures in the neck or back are very serious, and improper transportation may cause great increase in severity. If the patrolman finds that he must transport the victim, he would not apply splints to the back. He would probably lay the man on his back on a door or a firm frame shaped like a door. Or he might transport him lying on the stomach on a stretcher.

Question: An old woman has a bad fall. She says that she thinks her hip is broken. What is a fracture of the hip?

Answer: It usually refers to a fracture near the upper end of the

---

* *To the teacher:* Although not a usual part of the junior course, a brief explanation of splinting or other first aid measures for fractures of the backbone, arm, and thigh bones may be given if time permits.

thigh bone. Fractures of any part of the thigh bone are extremely serious. Always get help in such cases.

Question: A boy caught a ball on the tips of his fingers. The finger joints swelled and became painful. What is the proper first aid?

Answer: Apply cold cloths immediately. Keep the fingers and hand quiet. Be sure to have X-rays, because fractures may be present.

Question: What is the first aid for a broken nose?

Answer: Usually nothing should be done to the nose before taking the victim to a doctor. If a wound is present, apply a sterile dressing.

FIRST AID AND ARITHMETIC

If the present accident injury rate continues, 1 person in every 13 will have a disabling injury next year. (A disabling injury is one that is severe enough to cause loss of time from work, school, or usual activity *beyond* the day of injury.)

1. Suppose a school has 1,004 students. How many disabling injuries will the students have next year at the above rate?

2. People who study first aid usually have fewer accidents because they then become more careful. Supposing the reduction is one-third, what would the reduction in the number of disabling injuries be next year in the school described above if all the students studied first aid and became more careful?

3. How many disabling accidents would the students in your school have next year if the rate is 1 per 13 students?

4. If the students in your school all study first aid and have a reduction of one-third in accidents, how many disabling accidents would be prevented?

5. At 1 disabling accident per 13 people, find how many such accidents will happen in your city next year. (If you live on a farm, find the answer for a nearby city or for your county.)

6. In 1 recent year in the United States 9,825 children from 10 through 14 years old died. The most important causes of these deaths were: accidents, 3,243; heart disease, 850; pneumonia, 634; appendicitis, 517; tuberculosis, 496. What percent of all deaths were caused by accidents? Accidents caused how many times as many deaths as heart disease? Make other arithmetic problems or graphs from the figures.

REVIEW QUESTIONS

1. What is a joint?
2. What is a dislocation?
3. Tell what to do for a dislocation.
4. What is a sprain?
5. What are signs of a sprain?
6. Tell what to do for a sprained ankle.

12

A GENERAL PLAN
FOR GIVING FIRST AID

Thus far you have learned about many kinds of injuries. When you see a person who has just been injured, it is wise to have a plan by which you proceed in giving the proper first aid.

First check quickly to learn whether the victim has injuries requiring speedy first aid. There are three kinds of cases like this. Is there *severe bleeding?* Is the case one that requires *artificial respiration?* Is the case one of *poisoning?* Give first aid immediately to cases of these three kinds, following methods you have already studied, because they are the "hurry cases" of first aid.

Most cases do not require such speedy action; instead, haste may be very harmful. If your first quick view shows that you are not dealing with a hurry case, have the victim lie down and cover him properly if the injury seems serious. Then summon help.

In some cases it may be important to learn something about the injuries or illness before you call for help. Ask the victim what he thinks is wrong. Try to find what happened to him. Did he fall? If so, how far? Was he struck? If so, by what object and in what body part? Examine him cautiously. Is he unconscious? Can you see bruises, bleeding, evidence of fracture, burns? A mistake sometimes made by first aiders is that after finding one injury they fail to examine for others. Another possible mistake is that upon finding several injuries they may give first aid only for the worst one and neglect the others.

After you have made your examination, if you must do something besides summoning help, you should take time to think and plan what to do. Many errors in first aid occur because the helpers rush into action before planning carefully. Most accident and illness cases are not hurry cases. Take time to do good work. After

making your plans, collect the material you will need, assign tasks to each helper so that he knows exactly what to do, and then go ahead with care, remembering that what you do at this time may be exceedingly important. During your planning do not disturb the victim unnecessarily.

Sometimes the excitement at the scene of accident or sudden illness disturbs the first aider so much that he does not do good work. A large crowd may gather. The victim may be in great pain. Blood may be seen here and there. Perhaps the victim or his relatives may be sobbing and demanding rush action. Often someone in the crowd wants to do things you know to be wrong. For instance, he may want to rush the victim away without learning anything about the injuries, without stopping blood flow or splinting fractures. Sometimes, if the injury occurs in very cold weather, darkness, or rain, or in busy city life, the first aider may, because of these circumstances, decide to follow wrong methods. But if you are a good first aider, you will keep calm and will not be disturbed by unfavorable conditions or by people who give incorrect advice. You will, instead, be of real help to the person in distress.

PRACTICAL WORK

Stage a play, showing the value of planning in case of an accident. Cast members may read their parts.

CAST: *Mark, Harold, Verne, Philip.*

SCENE: *A ski slide in mountain country.*

EQUIPMENT NEEDED: *A clean handkerchief, a scout neckerchief or a triangular bandage, 3 coats, a light rope.*

SCENE ONE

(*Pretend that Mark, Harold, and Verne are standing at the foot of the hill, looking toward the top.*)

MARK: I can see Phil now. He's getting ready to ski down.

HAROLD: Phil certainly takes chances. Some day he'll get hurt or he'll hurt someone else.

VERNE: He's the best skier around here.

HAROLD: Yes, but when a person is pretty good he may think he's better. That's why some good athletes have their share of accidents.

MARK: Here he comes. Look, he's trying to jump the ditch!

VERNE: Boy, is he taking a chance!

MARK: Well, this time he's taking one chance too many—see, he's lost his balance!

HAROLD: Mark, he's fallen—hit his head on that rock. Come on, hurry—let's go over.

(End of Scene One)

SCENE TWO

(Philip is lying on his back, evidently in pain. The other three boys run toward him.)

VERNE: Quick, see whether he's bleeding.

MARK: Yes, he's got a cut on the forehead.

VERNE: Stop the bleeding at once—that's good first aid. Where's a cloth to use for direct pressure?

HAROLD: Here's a handkerchief.

VERNE: It's not clean. Used handkerchiefs have lots of germs on them. Anybody have a clean handkerchief or cloth?

MARK: I have—here it is.

(Verne applies pressure against the wound on Philip's forehead.)

VERNE: Now where's something I can use as a cravat bandage?

MARK: Here, take this scout neckerchief.

(Verne applies the cravat head bandage.)

HAROLD: Well, now let's see. We took care of the hurry angle.

MARK: That's right. We stopped the bleeding and we don't have any artificial respiration or poisoning to deal with.

HAROLD: What's next? Now we don't need to hurry.

VERNE: Keep him lying down. Cover him. Get help.

MARK: Shall we get help first?

VERNE: It will take quite a while. And it's cold here.

MARK: All right. I'll throw my coat over him.

(Mark does so.)

Mark continues: Before we slide a coat under him, we ought to know what part is hurt. Phil, are you hurt anywhere else?

PHILIP: Yes, I've got a backache, and my right ankle hurts.

(Mark examines Philip gently. He looks at the head, runs his hand along the upper extremities, the trunk, thighs, and legs. As he does so, he asks Philip whether the part touched is tender; Philip answers "No" each time till Mark touches the right ankle.)

MARK: Is this where the ankle hurts?

PHILIP: Yes. I think it's broken.

MARK: It's swelling a little. Where does your back hurt?

PHILIP: About the middle of the back, just below the ribs.

HAROLD: He might have some trouble there. Let's slide an overcoat under him.

VERNE: Maybe we should splint the ankle first.

PHILIP: Perhaps it's only a sprain.

HAROLD: When in doubt, play the safe side. That means splint.

MARK: Let's see—where do the splints go for a broken ankle?

VERNE: The important rule is this: Keep the broken ends and the nearby joints quiet. Doing that in any way is good first aid. We can put a splint on each side, running from the heel to just below the knee. Maybe we could use the skis.

HAROLD: Yes, or we can wrap a coat around the ankle. Verne, let me use your coat because you've got a sweater under it. I don't have any triangular bandages, but I do have some light rope in my pocket.

(Harold folds a coat and applies it to the ankle.)

MARK: Now we can slide Harold's coat under Philip. Let's be very careful. Don't twist his back. I'll keep his ankle quiet.

(The boys slide the coat under Philip.)

HAROLD: Now I'll go for help. There's a farmhouse about half a mile away. If they can't help, I'll telephone for the ski patrol. They know first aid.

MARK: You may need a nickel for a telephone call.

HAROLD: I've got a nickel. Phil, do you think you're worth that much of my money? Oh, Verne, while I'm gone, why don't you two get some poles for a stretcher?

(Harold leaves.)

PHILIP: It was all my fault, trying to show off. And I'm a good skier. Every little kid around here watches me. Now all I show them is how to break a leg.

Verne: Cheer up, Phil. We'll have you in a warm bed in no time. You just lie quiet. Mark and I are going to sit down on the log over there and plan what to do next.

Philip: I'll lie quiet all right, wondering how much this will cost and how my foot will be.

Mark: Now, Phil, take it easy. You know that might be a sprain, not a break. We'll be back before long.

(End of play)

REVIEW QUESTIONS

1. What are the "hurry cases" of first aid?
2. List ways by which you can learn about the injuries of an accident victim.
3. List in order what steps to take in case someone is injured.
4. Is a person who has a broken bone a "hurry case"?

13

MOVING INJURED
OR SICK PERSONS

If you encounter a seriously injured or sick person, it is usually best to get help before moving him. Improper methods of transportation frequently make the injury worse and can even cause death. Haste is usually unnecessary and often harmful.

Sometimes an injured person lies in a location dangerous to his life, such as on a heavily traveled highway or in a burning, wrecked automobile. Even here, adults are usually nearby, and you should quickly summon help. In cases like these the victim often has a fracture; yet perhaps it is necessary to move him a short distance to safety before applying splints. You can see how dangerous it is to the victim to move him unsplinted from a wrecked car or a highway. "Splint 'em where they lie," if possible. You might save a life by quickly calling for help and by warning oncoming traffic. But, meanwhile, stay off the roadway yourself; play safe.

A really excellent way of transporting is by stretcher. It is safe for the victim. If a stretcher is not available, you can make one, as shown later. A door makes a solid stretcherlike support. Or a ladder with a mattress, or *several boards nailed together into stretcher shape will be satisfactory*. A stretcher can be placed in an automobile, but the first aiders should practice first how to do it.

Of course, it is much better to place the stretcher in an ambulance or truck. Often the best method of transportation proves, finally, to be the *cheapest*.

PRACTICAL WORK

Equipment needed: Stretcher poles, blanket, coats or vests.

1. **Practice the walking assist.**

This is a method of helping a person who has a bruised or sprained foot. Take hold of him as shown in the illustration.

2. **Make a stretcher from materials you can find.** The following suggestions may help:

a. Two poles and a blanket may be used.

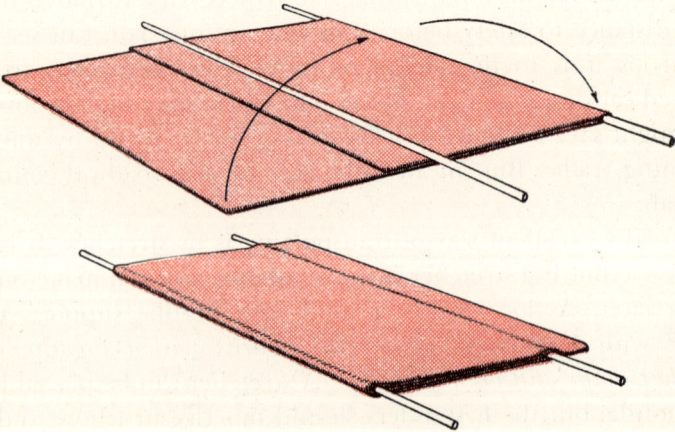

b. A blanket rolled up at the edges makes a fairly good stretcher. It is not as good as a stretcher having poles.

c. Two poles and a few coats or vests. A stretcher may be made as illustrated, but is not always very good. Try to make one and see why the coats or vests must be carefully selected.

3. **Slide a blanket under a pretended victim.**

4. **Load a class member upon a stretcher.**

Use four people besides the victim. Three place themselves on one side of the victim, the fourth on the other side.

The three bearers each kneel on the knee nearest the victim's feet. They pass their hands under the victim.

At the command "Ready, lift!" from the fourth person, the bearers lift the victim, placing him upon their knees. The fourth person then slides the stretcher in front of the bearers. At the command of "Lower!" the victim is gently placed upon the stretcher.

The lifting of a sick or injured person is not as easy as it may seem. Even in practice work, you should be very careful so that you do not strain your back or drop the victim.

5. **Now practice carrying with a stretcher.**

The four bearers should place themselves as shown in the drawing. One bearer should be assigned to say "Ready, lift!" The front and side bearers step off with the left foot; the rear bearer steps off with the right foot.

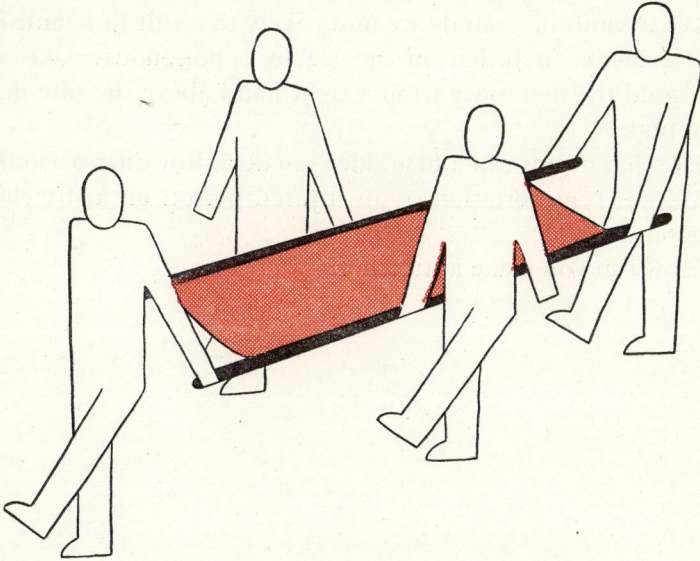

PROBLEMS

1. Three kinds of work in which many accidents occur are farming, mining, and lumbering. List several reasons why farmers, even more than most city people, need to know about first aid.

2. Many farmers and their family members do not know first aid. Suppose you live on a farm or in a farming community. Make a list of ways by which you can interest farmers or farm children in learning first aid.

3. A student in the eighth grade wants to drive the family automobile. The father says he will not give permission until a

first aid course has been studied. He gives reasons for his decision. Write a narrative presenting the conversation between the student and his father.

REVIEW QUESTIONS

1. In what kinds of accidents should you give first aid for shock?
2. What is proper first aid for shock?
3. List ways to stop bleeding.
4. How should nosebleed be stopped?
5. What is meant by first aid?
6. What kinds of wounds are most likely to result in tetanus?
7. If someone is bitten on the leg by a poisonous snake, why should the first aider wrap a tight band above the bite marks at once?
8. By what means can a first aider rescue a drowning person?
9. Why is transportation of an injured person on a stretcher a good method?
10. How can you make a stretcher?

14

INJURIES DUE TO HEAT AND COLD

BURNS

Burns are injuries caused by contact with dry or moist heat, electricity, chemicals, or the sun's rays. Burns due to moist heat—steam or hot liquids—are called scalds. Chemicals, if they injure the skin, cause a special kind of burn called a chemical burn.

Danger of Burns

Burns are among the worst of all injuries. They heal slowly. The burned body part often becomes infected. Frequently burns require long hospitalization. When the body is badly burned, the victim may have pain for months when he moves about in bed or even when he lies quietly on the burned part. Burns sometimes disfigure the face badly. They sometimes result in permanent injury to those important instruments, the hands. A serious burn may cause hundreds or even thousands of dollars of expense in hospital and medical care.

Burns are a frequent cause of death. They are a particular source of danger to babies, school children, and old people.

Among children under 5 years of age, burns are the leading cause of accidental death. What a tragic way for a young child to die!

First Aid for Burns

In *mild* burns the skin becomes red but is not destroyed. Infection usually does not develop if the skin is not scratched or cut. For first aid, apply a burn ointment to the reddened parts. If the burn is very slight, pain may be decreased by putting the burned part at once in cold, clean water for a few moments before applying the ointment. For example, hold the part under running water from the faucet. Do not give first aid to burns by applying more heat. Any burn affecting much skin is serious even though the area is only reddened. Pain is great and shock may occur.

Sometimes part of the burned area develops blisters. In these cases infection is more likely. Do not break blisters open. When blistering is present, the best first aid lies in applying a sterile dressing and sending the patient to the doctor.

In deeper burns the skin is destroyed. The danger of infection is great. For first aid, apply a sterile dressing and bandage; *attend carefully to shock*. Sterile compresses wet with baking soda solution, 3 tablespoonfuls to a quart of warm water, may be applied if medical care is delayed.

Chemical Burns

In case a chemical is spilled on the skin, thoroughly wash the part at once in clean water. Tap water or a drinking fountain spray may be used. If the skin is only reddened, apply a burn ointment. If the burn is deeper, put on a sterile dressing.

If the chemical gets into the eye, wash the eye immediately and repeatedly with clean water. Then consult the doctor. Chemical injuries of the eye, even though they seem unimportant at first, may be very serious.

Sunburn

For sunburn, apply a burn ointment if the skin is reddened. If blisters are present, do not break them, but apply a sterile dressing before getting further care. Severe sunburn causes swelling of the skin, a fever, and headache.

INJURIES DUE TO COLD

A frostbitten part of the body should be covered snugly until the victim can get indoors. Rub the skin *surrounding* the frostbitten part, but *not* the part itself. If the feet are badly affected, take off the shoes, wrap the feet warmly and have the victim lie down with the feet raised somewhat while you are transporting him.

Once indoors, do not rub the frozen part with snow or anything else. Loosen tight clothing, cover the frozen part moderately, and rub the body parts surrounding it. Use your hands or a towel. Formerly it was not believed wise to bring the victim immediately into a warm room, but now we know that he can immediately be brought into a room heated to about 70°.

If a person is badly chilled throughout his body by exposure to the cold, he should be brought indoors, put to bed, covered, and given warm drinks. Gently rubbing his limbs and face may help. Keep him away from people who have colds or other infections.

PRACTICAL WORK

Carries

There are various ways to carry a victim. Do not injure yourself by trying to lift a person who is too heavy. Lift slowly, keeping your back rather straight. Use your thigh muscles rather than your back muscles. In industries in which heavy lifting is done, the safety director always teaches the workers the right way to lift. Even in classroom practice be careful and safe.

Carry by Extremities

This method is used for victims of fainting and other conditions when no serious injury is present. Don't use it in fracture cases.

Four-Hand Seat

The four-hand seat can be used with conscious people. This method usually is not as good as the carry by extremities.

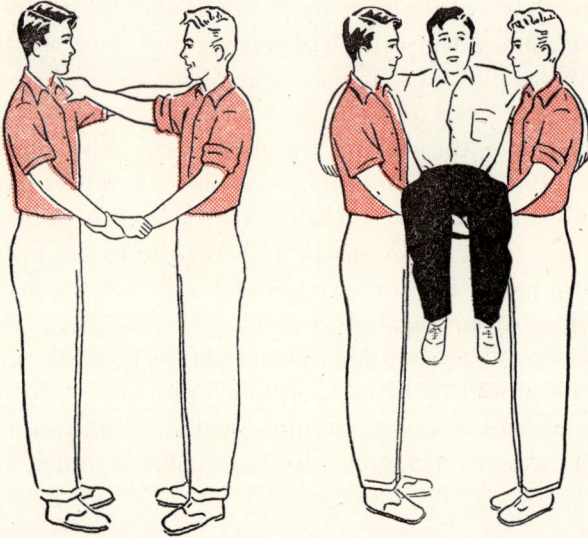

Pack-Strap Carry

The pack-strap carry is the best one-man carry. The victim's armpits should be well up on the first aider's shoulders. The first aider can grasp both of the victim's hands with one of his hands, leaving the other free to open doors. This carry is not good in case of fractures.

Three-Man Carry

This carry resembles the one practiced for use in loading a stretcher. The bearers walk side step after lifting the victim. Practice it. Observe that this carry is not as easy to do well as you may have thought.

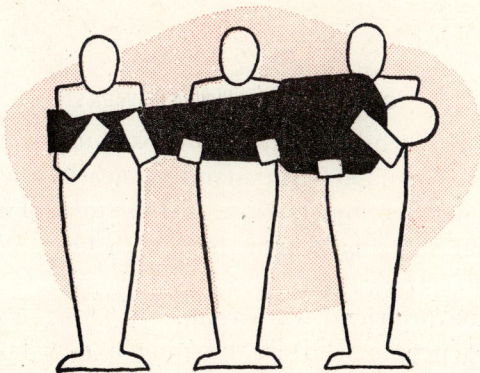

Eight-Man Carry

Practice also the eight-man carry, four people on each side of the victim; with the hands alternated as shown.

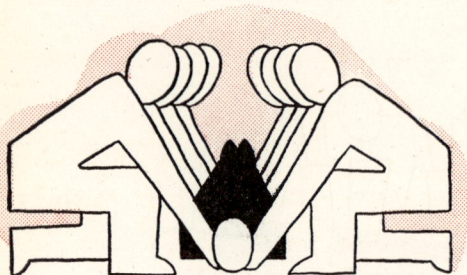

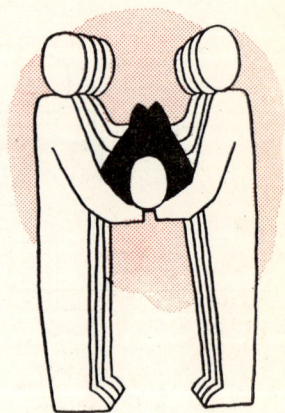

QUESTIONS AND ANSWERS

Question: A girl, while learning to cook, burned her fingers on a hot pan. A friend standing nearby then told her to bring her fingers close to the stove. The friend said that she should treat heat with heat. Was the friend correct?

Answer: No, the friend was wrong.

Question: Do people who are learning a new task have more accidents than experienced people?

Answer: Yes. When you start a new job, be especially careful. For example, girls learning to cook or iron often have several burn spots, just as boys learning to play football or to do carpenter work often have more than their share of bruises and cuts.

Question: What is the commonest cause of accidental death among babies?

Answer: Suffocation. Perhaps the baby lies on his stomach with his face buried in the pillow so that the air is shut off, or the baby's mother may not have learned to cover her child properly. The danger of suffocation is greater if the mother or someone else sleeps with the baby.

Question: Does a person get a sunburn more quickly if he is at a high altitude—for example, in the mountains—rather than at sea level?

Answer: Yes.

Question: A baby pulled on the tablecloth, upsetting a pot of coffee. The baby was scalded. Could such a burn lead to death?

Answer: Sometimes a scald caused in this way leads to a baby's death.

REVIEW QUESTIONS

1. Name some common ways by which buildings and forests catch fire.
2. Why are burns such serious injuries?
3. What is the proper first aid for a small burn in which the skin becomes red?
4. What is the proper first aid if a burned part has blisters?
5. What should you do if you spill a chemical on the skin?
6. What should you do if a chemical gets into the eye?
7. How long should you stay in the sun if you do not have a sun tan?
8. How can you decrease the chance of getting sunburned?
9. What first aid should be given in case of sunburn?
10. What first aid should be given in case of frostbite?

15

UNCONSCIOUSNESS

Accidents or illnesses sometimes result in unconsciousness. An injury to the brain because of a blow on the head is called a *concussion*. If severe, it may cause unconsciousness. Most people who become unconscious following an automobile accident or following a fall in which the head is struck are suffering from *concussion*. Sometimes interference with the blood supply to the brain occurs in older people, and they have a stroke, becoming unconscious. People may become unconscious because of severe bleeding, drinking alcohol, taking poisons, or because of heart disease and many other illnesses or injuries.

First Aid

In case of unconsciousness, first find whether the victim is breathing. If not, you should give artificial respiration, provided the victim's condition was caused by drowning or some other type of accident for which artificial respiration is recommended. Cases of stroke and of concussion are, in general, not helped by artificial respiration, even though the person has stopped breathing.

If, as is usually the case, the victim does not need artificial respiration, you should provide covering above and below him. Be careful, because a broken bone may be present. If the victim's face is red or purplish, raise the head and shoulders slightly by pillows or other supports. If the face is pale, the victim should lie flat. Do not try to arouse an unconscious person by shouting at him, shaking him, or throwing water upon him. Let him lie undisturbed while you summon help.

SIMPLE FAINTING

People who are in crowded rooms, who are hungry, tired, fearful, or see blood may faint even though they are in good health. The immediate cause is an insufficient supply of blood to the brain. As soon as they lie flat, they recover consciousness, because then the brain gets enough blood.

Prevention

If you feel faint, bend forward at the waist, bringing the head down between the knees. Or better yet, lie down.

First Aid

Keep the victim lying flat. If he gets up soon, he may faint again. Loosen his collar. After he recovers consciousness, a drink of tea or coffee may bring further relief. If he does not recover very soon, the case is not one of simple fainting, and a doctor should be consulted.

EPILEPTIC CONVULSIONS

Many people suffer from an illness called epilepsy. In this illness they may have an epileptic convulsion; that is, they become unconscious, fall, and thrash around on the ground. Usually the attack ends quickly, but the patient may seem sleepy and confused for a time. Doctors can help these patients very much.

If a person has an epileptic attack, he may bite his tongue or injure himself by striking against something. Do not try to hold him, but see that he does not strike anything. If possible, place a folded cloth or a strong stick between the teeth so that he does not bite his tongue. But be very careful in doing this, lest he become injured.

After the attack, do not question the victim unless absolutely necessary. He should lie down undisturbed, and sleep.

PRACTICAL WORK

Stage a play dealing with un-consciousness. Unless directed otherwise by the teacher, have cast members read their parts.

CAST: *Edward, Fred, Howard, Mary Lou, Lucille, and on-lookers.*

EQUIPMENT NEEDED: *A water glass or cup.*

SCENE: *Near school play-ground. When the scene opens, Edward is lying on the ground near a roadway.*

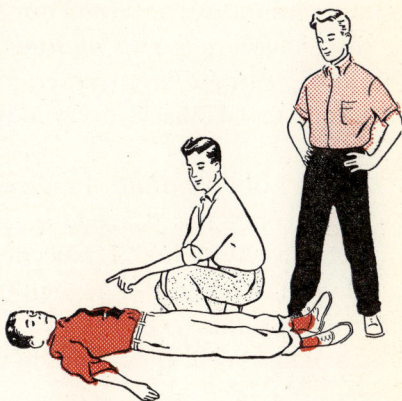

Fred and Howard appear, walking slowly and talking.

FRED: Look there, Howard. Someone is hurt!

HOWARD: Why, it's Ed! Wonder what happened to him.

FRED: Is he asleep or is he unconscious? Howard, there's some blood on the ground—coming from his scalp!

HOWARD: Well, then, he must be unconscious. He must have been hit by a car. Let's wake him up.

(Howard shakes him gently and shouts, "Ed, wake up." Meanwhile Mary Lou and Lucille enter the scene.)

MARY LOU: Is he hurt? Why, he's unconscious!

FRED: That's right. We're shaking him so that he'll wake up.

MARY LOU: No, you shouldn't do that. I'm taking first aid in school, and teacher says you shouldn't try to arouse an uncon-scious person. Just let him lie quiet.

LUCILLE: I'm going to get some water.

(Lucille runs off stage and returns at once with a glass of water. Meanwhile Mary Lou looks carefully at the head wound.)

LUCILLE: Look out, Mary Lou, I'm going to throw some water in his face.

MARY LOU: No, don't do that either. There's no reason to pour water on an unconscious person unless he was overcome by heat.

HOWARD: Well, everybody does it. I've seen people do it.

MARY LOU: Yes, but most people don't know first aid. Let me examine him a little.

(Meanwhile a group of students enter the scene and gather around Edward. They are excited.)

LUCILLE: Get back, everybody. Give him air. He needs lots of air.

MARY LOU: *(Smiling)* It seems that whenever there's an accident, someone says, "Give him air."

LUCILLE: Why not? He needs air, doesn't he?

MARY LOU: Yes, but he won't suffocate because there are people around him.

LUCILLE: Well, they shouldn't come up too close to him anyhow.

MARY LOU: That's right. They interfere with the examination and get in the way.

HOWARD: What if you're indoors—wouldn't you open the windows?

MARY LOU: I might if the room were stuffy. But I wouldn't chill a sick person by letting cold air blow over him.

(At this point Edward moves slightly and groans.)

LUCILLE: There—he moved! I'm going to pour this water down his throat.

FRED: No, I know *that's* wrong. Never give water to an unconscious person. It might get into his windpipe.

LUCILLE: Well, he moved a little, so he isn't unconscious.

MARY LOU: Unconscious people sometimes move or mumble. Don't give water to drink till he's completely conscious and says he can swallow.

(Edward takes a rather deep breath.)

HOWARD: Did you notice that? I think he's gasping. I'm going to lift him up and down.

(Howard grasps Edward by the belt and attempts to lift him but is restrained by Mary Lou.)

MARY LOU: Howard, that's wrong, too. I suppose you think all I can say is "don't." But that is the trouser belt lift, and it's no good.

HOWARD: I've seen it done in football when somebody has the wind knocked out of him.

MARY LOU: Maybe you have. But it's still wrong. The person may have a broken back or damage to his liver or other organs. You can hurt him very much by this lifting.

HOWARD: But if he's gasping, he needs air.

MARY LOU: Of course. But as long as he gasps he gets it. Let him lie quietly. This is a head injury. And you see his face is flushed; so it is *red* unconsciousness. He needs a dressing on the scalp wound. And his head and shoulders should be raised a little. Maybe he has some broken bones. But let's call the coach to help. There he comes now. The most important thing for unconsciousness is quiet.

(End of play)

QUESTIONS AND ANSWERS

Question: If your clothes catch fire, what should you do?

Answer: Roll up in a blanket or rug to smother the flames. Or if such material is not at hand, lie down and roll over slowly. Try to beat out the flames with your hands or, better yet, with any cloths you can reach. Don't run, for thereby you fan the flames. Don't stand up, for if you do you will breathe the hot air and flame, and your face will be burned.

Question: Is the air in a burning room hottest near the ceiling?

Answer: Yes, usually. Therefore, keep low in a burning room.

Question: A man is trapped in a burning building, but his own room is not yet on fire. What should he do?

Answer: He should quickly close the doors and windows in the room. Then he should decide how to escape. Perhaps he can climb out through a window. People often jump from high buildings and are killed. If they had remained in a tightly closed room, they might have been rescued by firemen. While they wait, they might open one of the windows a few inches and breathe the fresh air. Perhaps they can cover the face with a wet cloth if there is a faucet in the room.

Perhaps there is an escape down a hallway or other passage. But before opening the door to find out, the trapped person should feel the door to find whether it is hot. He should keep very low when opening the door, and brace himself, because the strong hot-air currents may force the door wide open. Many trapped people are killed when they open a door because they breathe the hot air. One breath of very hot air may be enough to cause great injury. Also, hot air often contains carbon monoxide, which is poisonous.

Question: What parts of the body should be particularly guarded from the flame?

Answer: The face and the hands. You know how harmful the burns of the face may be, and how important it is to avoid breathing hot air. Protect your hands especially, too, for they are very important instruments. Covering the head with a coat or towel will protect it somewhat against flame. Such covering does not protect against carbon monoxide, however.

A TRUE STORY

A mother was cleaning clothes with a cleaning fluid that was *inflammable*. While she rubbed, using the fluid, the clothes suddenly burst into flame. Then her dress caught fire. Meanwhile her two little children became frightened and ran to her. Their clothes caught fire also. All three suffered extensive burns of the face and body, and the mother died soon after.

In cases of very large burns like these, the best first aid would be to wrap large sheets around the body; then cover well and call a doctor quickly.

A good rule: Do not use an inflammable cleaning fluid. (Note that "inflammable" and "flammable" both mean the same thing: "capable of being easily set on fire.")

PROBLEMS

1. Make a list of ways by which harmful fires are started.
2. Make a list of ways by which little children suffer burns.
3. If you live on a farm, write what you can do to prevent fires.

REVIEW QUESTIONS

1. List some causes of unconsciousness.
2. What is the proper first aid for unconsciousness?
3. What should be done to prevent simple fainting?
4. What is the proper first aid for simple fainting?
5. Describe the proper first aid for epileptic convulsions.

16

COMMON ILLNESSES;
FIRST AID KITS

ABDOMINAL PAIN

Abdominal pain should not be dismissed lightly for it may be caused by a serious disease, such as appendicitis. Too often, in case of abdominal pain, people postpone calling a doctor and give extremely harmful first aid by administering a laxative. Then, if the trouble is appendicitis, the appendix may rupture, and even more serious illness or death may follow.

The proper first aid lies in putting the victim to bed, withholding food, and getting medical care. A laxative should not be given. Always play the safe side in case of abdominal pain.

BLISTERS CAUSED BY PRESSURE

It is best if you do not open blisters caused by pressure, such as may develop on the feet from wearing tight shoes, or on the hands from rowing a boat or chopping wood. Wash the part gently and have someone apply a sterile dressing.

BOILS AND PIMPLES

Keep the surrounding skin clean by gentle washing with soap and water. *Do not squeeze boils or pimples.* Those about the nose, eyes, and upper lip are especially dangerous. Boils should be treated by a doctor.

COLDS

In the United States the most common disease caused by germs is the ordinary cold. It is unfortunate that many people think this illness is trivial. Colds often pave the way for more serious disease. Germs in the body that previously could not get a foothold sometimes grow rapidly when the body is weakened by a cold. Then such diseases as pneumonia, sinus infection, and ear infection may develop. In recent years progressive people have given much more attention to the care of their colds.

Prevention

Keep away from those with colds. If you cannot keep entirely away, stay as far away as you can. For instance, if you ride in an automobile with someone who has a cold, you are very likely to catch it. Wash your hands before eating. Wear clothing that is sufficiently warm. Eat proper food. Get plenty of rest. Guard against chilling, particularly after active play or hard work. After washing the hair and scalp, dry it thoroughly and stay indoors several hours.

First Aid

The most important first aid measure when one has a cold is to rest, preferably in bed. Many people claim that certain medicines and home remedies cure colds. Some of them may make a person feel somewhat better while he is ill. For instance, headache tablets, cold pills, laxatives, heating pads, and mustard plasters may give some relief from discomfort, but it is doubtful whether they hurry the healing process. You may be benefited somewhat if you eat lightly and drink more fluid than usual. It is unwise to treat a cold by "working up a sweat."

CRAMPS OF THE EXTREMITIES

For first aid, have the victim lie down. Apply hot, wet towels and massage the affected muscles, stroking toward the trunk. The same first aid helps in case a foot falls asleep.

PRACTICAL WORK

1. **Examine the contents of a first aid kit.**

Every kit should contain some 1-inch adhesive dressings, some sterile dressings of medium size, 4 x 4 inches, and others of large size, burn ointment, antiseptic, and triangular bandages. A tourniquet may also be included.

Many kits also contain ammonia, which was once thought to be helpful for fainting and weakness. Now many doctors believe it has little real value. It is not included in Red Cross kits.

2. **Give a play telling about first aid equipment.** Cast members may read their parts. This playlet might, instead, be presented as a radio play.

CAST: *Larry, Joan, Patricia, Allen.*

SCENE: *Schoolroom.*

EQUIPMENT: *Chairs for cast members, cardboard or wooden box, dressings, bandages, burn ointment, antiseptic, splints, flashlight, jackknife, blanket, flares. If make-believe items are used, they should be prepared beforehand and labeled in large print.*

LARRY: It's getting close to the end of our first aid course. I wonder whether we'll have an examination.

JOAN: I suppose so. That seems to be a part of school.

PATRICIA: We'll have to take examinations if we want Red Cross certificates.

LARRY: I wonder how hard it will be. Why are there such things as examinations?

PATRICIA: You sound as though you think schools and school teachers are against you. But they're working for you so that you can earn some money and have a good job and enjoy life and help your community.

ALLEN: I must admit that I wouldn't study so hard if we never had exams.

LARRY: What questions will we have if we do have an exam?

JOAN: Oh, something about shock and bleeding for sure. Something about broken bones, too.

ALLEN: Maybe teacher will ask what to do if we see an automobile accident.

LARRY: What can you do if you don't have dressings and bandages?

ALLEN: Perhaps if you look in the wrecked car you can find a first aid kit, or you might be in a car yourself and have one.

PATRICIA: With so much chance of having an accident, it's strange that so many people don't have first aid kits in their cars.

JOAN: Maybe the kits cost too much money.

PATRICIA: Fiddlesticks! A kit doesn't have to cost very much. You can make one easily.

JOAN: I'm going to make my dad put one in our car.

ALLEN: *Make* him do it? How?

JOAN: Oh, I have ways. I can approach him in a certain way, and he'll do it.

PATRICIA: I'm going to make a kit myself.

LARRY: How?

PATRICIA: Oh, I'll get a shoe box or a grocery box and make some triangular bandages myself and buy some dressings.

LARRY: I think a shoe box is too small. Get a box at least twice that big and have a good cover.

JOAN: Patricia, is that all you'll put in the first aid box?

PATRICIA: No, I'll get some burn ointment and fold a triangular bandage so that it can be used as a tourniquet.

ALLEN: I think that would be fun. There probably are some other things that ought to be in the car too, for instance, a bottle of antiseptic.

LARRY: I certainly would want some splints in the car. If I had a broken leg and didn't have splints, someone might come along and load me into a car unsplinted.

PATRICIA: Yes, or they might use a fence post or a branch of a tree. Those might be better than nothing, but they're not as good as a good splint.

LARRY: Of course not. And if I had a splint in the car, I could tell anyone who came along how to apply it, in case I was hurt.

ALLEN: You know there are other things that would help, too. Suppose the accident is at night. A flashlight would certainly be useful.

JOAN: That's right. Every car ought to have one. You can use it to warn traffic against driving into a wrecked or stalled car. And it helps in case of a flat tire at night.

PATRICIA: I decided that I want a jackknife, too. You have lots of use for a jackknife at an accident.

JOAN: It seems to me that a blanket, even an old one, is very important.

LARRY: Isn't your car heated?

JOAN: Yes, but if I'm hurt in a wrecked car, I hope someone will take me out of the car. The blanket might keep me warm, or it could be used as a stretcher.

ALLEN: Where will we put all these things?

PATRICIA: Put all the small items into the first aid box. Put the box and the blanket and splints into the trunk compartment.

LARRY: Well, let's see—there are the dressings, the bandages, burn ointment, antiseptic, and tourniquet. Then there are the flashlight, jackknife, blanket, and splints. Joan, you're a good writer. Won't you write the list on the blackboard so that I can remember the items better?

(Joan writes the list on the blackboard.)

ALLEN: You might add to that list two flares, or two red flags or reflectors.

JOAN: What are flares?

ALLEN: You can get them in many hardware and automobile supply stores. They don't cost much. In case a car is wrecked at night or stalled or you have a flat tire, your car might be struck by another car. Somebody could be killed or badly hurt. You might have to pay a lot of money in damages if you don't have flares or other signals out. Some flares are shaped like Roman candles and contain a lighting powder that burns for about 15 minutes. You place them beside the road, one about 100 feet in front of your stalled car and one about 100 feet in back to warn approaching traffic. You can even use them in daytime if your car is stalled on a curve. You have to be careful when you light them, because the flame shoots right out.

← 100 FT →   ← 100 FT →

PATRICIA: That's a good idea. Larry, what size should the splints be?

LARRY: I'd want at least two for the forearm or hand, about 3 inches wide, 17 inches long, and about ⅜ inches thick. I'd want at least two for the leg, about 3 or 4 inches wide and as long as would go into the trunk of the car—4½ feet long or even longer.

JOAN: I suppose in a lot of places the boys can make the splints in their manual training classes or in their homes.

ALLEN: I think the most important things for a car are the splints, the flashlight, the flares or red flags, and plenty of triangular bandages—six, at least.

PATRICIA: Well, I think we have all these items of equipment. Let's pack them into this box.

(*The other three class members help her pack the kit. Before placing each item in the container, the student shows it to the class, saying what it is.*)

JOAN: What shall we do with the big items?

PATRICIA: Let's just put them in a pile here.

(*The students finish placing the material.*)

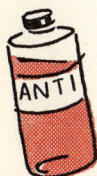

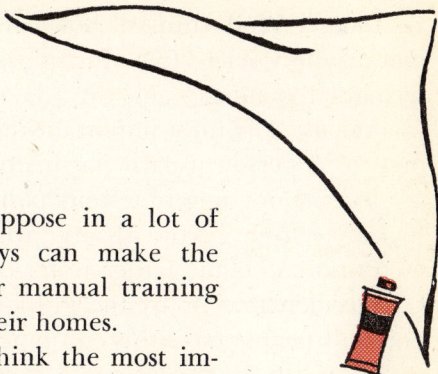

LARRY: Well, think of how easy this is to save serious trouble and maybe worse! How much does this all cost if you make your triangular bandages and get a box like this?

ALLEN: The most important things can be bought for a dollar or two. A person usually has many of them around the house.

JOAN: I'm going to tell my father about this. He's always talking safety to me. Now it's my turn to convince him.

PATRICIA: If my father won't equip our car, I'll do it myself. Car accidents occur by the millions, and he may be next. Why don't all people have this equipment?

LARRY: It isn't the expense. It's just that they never get around to doing the job.

ALLEN: That's right. We're all sure to see accidents some time, even if we're not in one. It's plain foolish not to have splints, bandages, flares, and a flashlight in a car. It reminds me of the scout motto: "Be Prepared."

(End of play)

PROBLEMS

1. Write a play about safety or first aid. Choose your own topic or select one from the following.

  a. Pretend that two or more students are preparing for an examination. Write their conversation about the examination and write the questions and answers they give each other about *one* of these subjects: shock, bleeding, poisoning, snake bite, burns, or drowning.

  b. Pretend that two people are talking about dangerous places, dangerous tasks, machines, or other objects. For example, pretend that they are walking through your house pointing out danger spots, such as loose rugs, unlighted stairways, or faulty electrical equipment. Or if you know about farms, pretend that they are walking through a barn telling about dangers there and how they can be corrected.

2. Practice your play or one of those given in this book. Arrange to give the play as a part of the program at a meeting of any organization you wish. Perhaps you can develop interest in first aid among the organization members in this way. Perhaps you can give the play at a meeting of the 4-H Club, the parent-teacher association, a church group, civic organization, or farm group.

REVIEW QUESTIONS

1. Why are colds dangerous?
2. What can you do to prevent colds?
3. What is proper first aid for a cold?
4. Should you take a laxative in case of abdominal pain?
5. Why should one call a doctor very soon in case of abdominal pain?

17

OTHER COMMON ILLNESSES

EARACHE

Sometimes earache occurs following exposure to cold. In such case an electric pad or hot-water bottle applied against the ear gives relief.

Often earache is caused by an infection in a part of the ear called the middle ear. There is a passageway between the nose and middle ear so that in case of colds in the nose, germs sometimes reach the middle ear. The danger is greater if one blows the nose vigorously, particularly if he shuts one nostril and closes the mouth at the same time.

First Aid

Go to bed and care for the cold. Do not blow the nose improperly. Apply a hot-water bottle or an electric pad to the ear. If the heat so applied does not give relief, use cold applications instead. Ear infection should always be treated by a physician. Otherwise, more serious disease may develop, and partial deafness may result.

HICCUP

One of the best ways to stop hiccup is to lie down and rest. Sometimes the hiccup stops if you drink water slowly. Try breathing in and out of a bag that fits tightly over the mouth. Or take a half teaspoonful of baking soda in water and drink slowly.

INSECT AND TICK BITES

Cold water or ammonia water applications may relieve the itching. Or try a paste of baking soda and cold cream. Sometimes the tick or insect remains attached to the skin. Remove it from below without squeezing it. Ticks may spread dangerous diseases, Rocky Mountain spotted fever and tularemia, when they bite. Ask your doctor how to prevent the diseases if you may be exposed to ticks.

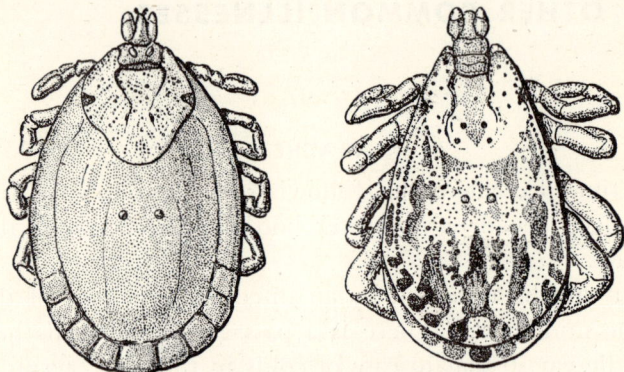

POISON IVY POISONING

Poison ivy, poison oak, and poison sumac frequently cause skin poisoning. It is possible that poison ivy and poison oak are really one kind of plant but grow differently under different soil and climate conditions.

Poison ivy and poison oak have shiny leaves that take on bright colors in the fall. Poison sumac leaves are orange colored early in spring; then they turn green. In the fall they become red-orange or russet color. The berries, when present, are white. The leaflets of poison ivy and poison oak are somewhat broad and grow in groups of three. Poison sumac usually has 7 to 13 leaflets in each group.

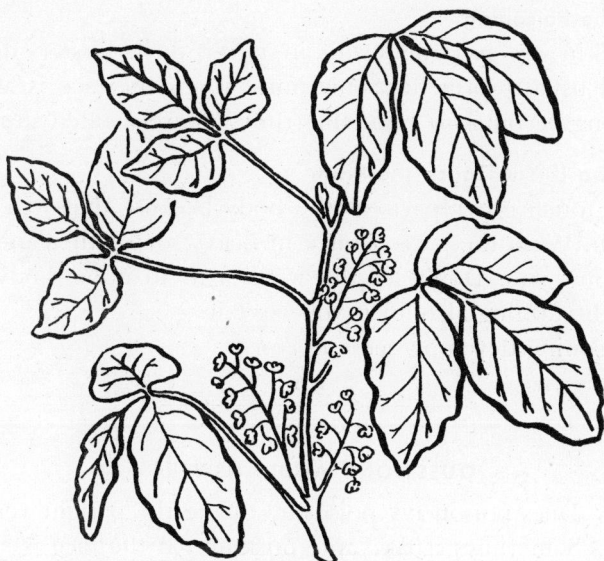

A good saying to remember is this:

Leaflets three—let it be;
Berries white—take fright.

Poison ivy grows as a low shrub, a crawling plant, or a climbing, vinelike plant. Poison oak is usually vinelike. It is not a tree. Poison sumac is a shrub or small tree, which may grow to a height of 20 feet. Sometimes these plants appear as a small cluster of leaves on stems only a few inches high.

How the Plants Cause Skin Poisoning

The plants form an oil. Tiny amounts, if placed on the skin, may cause severe poisoning. Some people are not poisoned as easily as others, but all people probably would be affected if they came in contact with enough oil. A person may have no effects from poison ivy one year and later be greatly bothered by a small amount. So take no chances.

Usually the poisoning results from touching the plant. But the amount needed to cause poisoning in some people is so small that they may suffer after touching a shoe that carries the oil. Even smoke from a burning plant may carry the oil.

Signs of the Poisoning

The skin gets red and swells in 1 to 9 days. Blisters develop. Itching is usually present. Sometimes, when the face is affected, the swelling becomes so great that the eyes are swollen shut.

What To Do If You Touch the Plant

Don't touch other parts of the body because that will spread the poison. Wash the part at once in heavy soap lather and warm water. Don't rub. Don't let the water run to other body parts. Rinse with rubbing alcohol if you have it.

If poisoning develops, see a doctor.

QUESTIONS AND ANSWERS

Question: Does poison ivy poisoning make the patient very sick?

Answer: Sometimes it does. For instance, if the face is affected, the swelling may be so great that the nose can hardly be seen. The patient is exceedingly uncomfortable and often must be sent to a hospital for treatment.

Question: Are boils caused by bad blood?

Answer: No. Boils are caused by germs that are rubbed into the skin and grow just beneath it. Pus in a boil contains millions of the germs. Boils often develop in the back of the neck because the collar rubs the germs down along the hair roots.

A TRUE STORY

A rancher and several cowboys were rounding up cattle in western New Mexico. The rancher was thrown from his horse, breaking a leg. He lay in a canyon several miles from a forest ranger's home. One of the cowboys went to the ranger for help. The ranger sent someone for the doctor, who lived 20 miles away. Meanwhile, he put a cracker box, a pillow, a blanket, bandages, and a small army-type cot into his truck and drove up the canyon toward the rancher. He could approach only part way because of trees. Then the ranger and the cowboy carried the cot and other equipment about 2 miles through the woods to the rancher.

The forest ranger broke out one end of the box. He placed the box at the foot of the bed and placed the pillow in it. Next he carefully applied the blanket around the injured leg. The cowboys helped him lift the rancher upon the bed. They placed the injured foot upon the pillow in the box. The forest ranger and three cowboys carried the cot and victim back to the truck. They had to avoid trees and rocks, and to cross a fast-flowing stream several times. When they returned to the truck, the doctor was waiting there.

The victim, after this trip in the canyon, was resting comfortably. The doctor said that exceptionally good first aid had been given. He thought that the use of the cot had saved the injured man much pain and had kept the broken bone ends motionless. When he examined the leg, he said that a sharp bone end was only an eighth of an inch beneath the skin. But the good first aid had prevented the simple fracture from becoming a compound one.

"What you did," he said, "took much time. But in serious accidents you should do everything right even though it does take time. No one has anything more important to do when an accident happens than saving a life or a limb."

REVIEW QUESTIONS

1. Describe the poison ivy and poison sumac plants.
2. Are all people poisoned if they touch poison ivy plants?
3. What should you do in case you touch poison ivy?
4. What should you do in case of hiccup? In case of insect bite?
5. Why is it dangerous to squeeze boils?
6. Suppose you telephone a doctor in case of an accident. What information would you give him?

INDEX